Do as I did
A Legacy

HANNAH D. LEITER

with

Ruth Leiter-Itzkowitz

Foreword by Yechiel Leiter

Printed in the United States of America

First Printing: 2017

Book design by Viviane Tubiana
Copy editing by Fraida Cohen

HDLeiter@gmail.com

ISBN: 0-9914488-4-7
ISBN-13: 978-0-9914488-4-5

DEDICATION

THIS BOOK IS DEDICATED to my children and grandchildren in the hope that they will benefit from the wisdom and experiences of their grandparents as they make their own life choices.

A brief incident that happened during my own childhood will serve to illustrate this point.

A European cousin who had recently come to America called to offer my dad a *yichus brief*, that is, a letter listing the names of famous ancestors. "We can be very proud of these people," she said, "so I am sure that you would like to know who they are and what they did."

My dad thanked her for the thoughtful offer, but said that he really had no interest in that letter. "I already know what I think of my ancestors," he said "what I really need to be concerned about is what they think of me."

I hope that my progeny too will be guided by this principle as they tell their offspring:

"You have every reason to be proud of your ancestors, but you must live the kind of life that will make them proud of you."

Hannah D. Leiter

TABLE OF CONTENTS

PART IV - SPEECH BY RABBI MAX MINTZ
On the Occasion of Dov's Bar Mitzvah

PART V – APPENDICES

FOREWORD

WHAT IS IT THAT MAKES US WHO WE ARE? Do our propensities for one character trait or another emanate from our biological makeup or from our upbringing? Or to use the colloquialism; are our ways of thinking and acting the result of *nature* or *nurture?*

While on a theoretical plane the question is an interesting one, its significance is hardly limited to the realm of theory and scientific research. If who we are has more to do with our hereditary composition than the early influences on our lives, then parenting, the educational system, the criminal justice system as well as the political system should look one way. If on the other hand our DNA is easily modified by our surroundings then all the above should look very different, as the persistent debates in a host of academic disciplines such as psychology, anthropology, criminology, economics, and political theory demonstrate.

The RAMBAM (Hilchot Dai'ot), plainly states that both are true, nature and nurture together contribute to an individual's identity; but what is of crucial importance is that neither are true to the extent that they cannot be overcome. In other words, we choose whether or not to be byproducts of our conditioning or the self-made individuals of our autonomous choices.

Overcoming our predispositions through choice is a process; it takes constant repetition until we get it right. The MAHARAL (Tiferet Yisrael, 4) refers to the Mitzvoth and the Halacha as ropes helping us climb out of a pit. The pit in his metaphor is clearly the place where a person is left exclusively to his or her behavioral tendencies and thought processes, the place beyond our control, unless molded in to proper form through repeated acts of free choice that create an alternative habit; not the habit of nature or nurture, but the habit of free choice.

Jewish identity is crafted much the same way; the Torah prescribes for us what it is that must be etched into our minds and hearts in order for us to be all we can be as loyal sons and daughters of our people. "*Zachor*" – remember, and "*al tishkach*" – do not forget, refer to constants we must forever be cognizant of. They envelope us, empower us, drive us, and make true believers out of us.

Some "*Chasidim* and *Anshei Maaseh*" repeat these "*zechirot*" that appear in the Torah every day.

"Remember this day, in which you came out from Mitzrayim." SHEMOT, 13; 3

Our Exodus from Egypt is our birth certificate; we carry it with us like a driver's license or a passport. The political theorist Niccolò Machiavelli wrote that in order to understand a people you must study their founding. Our founding was in rebellion against human demigods; the advent of our peoplehood coincided with freedom from human bondage.

"Remember the Sabbath day, to keep it holy" SHEMOT, 20; 8

The Sabbath day is to be kept Holy so we don't lose our freedom to the productivity of our own hands; so we dare not succumb to the tempting notion that the creative powers we have been blessed with are not gifts from Hashem but of our own making.

"Only take heed to thyself, and keep thy soul diligently, lest thou forget the things which thine eyes have seen, and lest they depart from your heart all the days of thy life: but teach them thy sons, and thy sons' sons – the day that thou stoodest before the LORD thy GOD in Horev…." DEVARIM, 4; 9-10

We must remember that it was not as individuals but as a nation that we stood at Sinai, a revelation witnessed and experienced by all, incorporated into our identity through obligation and collective responsibility.

"And thou shalt remember all the way which the LORD thy GOD led thee these forty years in the wilderness...." DEVARIM, 8; 2

"But thou shalt remember the LORD thy GOD: for it is He who gives thee power to get wealth...." DEVARIM, 8; 18

As it was Hashem who provided us with sustenance to survive the long desert journey to the Eretz Yisrael, we must not forget, that our industriousness and economic productivity is dependent on His will.

"Remember, and forget not, how thou didst provoke the LORD thy GOD to anger in the wilderness...." DEVARIM, 9; 7

"Remember what the LORD thy GOD did to Miryam by the way, after you were come out of Mizrayim" DEVARIM, 24; 9

We are to remember that our actions, as a nation and as individuals, have consequences, that reward and punishment is a basic tenet of faith in a living G-d, and in doing so we are reminded that despite our failings, repentance and forgiveness is possible.

"Remember what Amalek did to thee by the way, when you were come out of Mizrayim...." DEVARIM, 25; 17

"O my people, remember now what Balaq king of Mo'av devised, and what Bil'am, the son of Be'or answered him...." MICHAH, 6; 5

Were we not to remind ourselves constantly that there is nothing that can placate anti-Semitism other than our total disappearance the temptation to compromise our identity would be great; in never forgetting we reiterate the sheer futility in trying to become what we are not. We remember too that human history has a divine cadence we cannot always see and understand; that it is in Hashem's power to turn curses into blessings, that – *Netzach Yisrael Lo Yishaker.*

"If I forget thee O Yerushalyim, let my right hand forget her cunning." TEHILIM, 137;

Apparently a later addition to the list, perhaps by R' Yaakov Emden, closer to a time when so many of our nation began to forget that *Chutz La'aretz* is a religious abnormality, and gave a modern voice to R' Yehuda Halevi's admonition that the prayers for Tzion are nothing more that "cackles of a starling."

There is though, another "Zachor" that is curiously absent from the list of daily zechirot: "Zachor yemot olam, binuh shnot dor v'dor, she'al avicha v'yagedcha, zekeinecha v'yomru lach." Remember the days of old; reflect upon the years of [other] generations. Ask your father, and he will tell you; your elders, and they will inform you.

Apparently the directive to study history, our history in the context of world history, or perhaps world history in the context of Jewish history, is too general to be included in the list of conscious-inducing and identity-building ideas to constantly remember. Or perhaps the emphasis here is not so much in remembering as it is in an intergenerational discussion and learning process: "*she'al*" – ask the elders, and "*yomru*" – they will tell you.[1]

And if it is remembrance we are dealing with, it is imperative to remember that Jewish history began with the Avoth and Imahot, with the creation of family and all the tribulations involved therein. Family is both nature and nurture, it is the context in which we forge our identity, as individuals and as a nation.

---

[1] Perhaps it was from here that the English philosopher Edmund Burke defined the "social contract" at the root of democracy not just as rights and obligations vis a vis government, but as the commitment one generation must have for the ensuing generations.

This, I think is the proper context for the book before us, the history of the Scranton Mintz family, our grandparents *a"h* Zalman Dov and Sarah Zlata, that mom has so painstakingly compiled. I say painstakingly only because of the very many hours she has put into it, undeterred by the lonely endeavor of sifting through documents, collecting memories and committing them to writing. But because of the value she places on family, her respect and appreciation for family, it was a labor of love for her I am sure.

Knowing my mother a bit, I can also say that without a doubt it is also a labor of obligation, the obligation to tell the next generation and our progeny after us who Bubbie and Zaidy were, and how through them and their parents and their parents' parents, we too left Mitzrayim, and stood at Sinai, and mean it when we say *L'shana Habaa B'Yerushalayim.*

It is not only a story then of who they were, but of who we are; where our nature came from, what we have been nurtured, and most importantly, what we can choose to be.

Mom has done the *"Yomru"* it is now for us to do the *"Sheal"*.

Yechiel Leiter

PROLOGUE

Thursday
February 13, 1964

It was a crisp, cold winter morning and Dad stood in front of his place of business on Middle Street, waiting to say good-bye to us. Noson Zvi and I, Yechiel aged four and Hayim aged two and baby Gitti had just spent two wonderful weeks in Scranton and were on our way home to Rochester. Our vacation which was to have lasted a week had been extended another week for no reason other than the fact that we always found it hard to leave. As he bade us so long, Dad was his usual cheerful self, looking the picture of health, energized and ready for his usual day's work.

Shabbos Morning
February 15, 1964

At about 10:30AM, as I was involved in the usual duties of childcare and preparing *Shabbos* lunch, I was overtaken by a sudden and inexplicable fatigue and weakness. I needed to lie down. It was about thirty minutes before I was able to return to normal activity. The rest of the Shabbos passed without incident.

Directly after Shabbos
February 15, 1964

Noson Zvi took the call, and from the expression on his face, it was obvious that someone had died. "Just tell me that it isn't my father," I said. His answer, "I'm sorry, I can't tell you that."

How it happened was told to us by people who were actually there. After having recited the *Haftorah* in honor of his forthcoming *Yahrzeit* that week, Dad had stepped to the side of the *bima* to await the *Kel*

Moleh which the *Gabbai* would say. It was about 10:30AM. Suddenly, and without forewarning of any kind, Dad fell to the floor. There was an immediate call for an ambulance even though it was obvious to all present that he was gone as soon as he hit the floor. It was not to be believed that just minutes before he had completed the *Haftorah* as he had so many times before in Shul. Dad's *Haftorah* was something that people always found both inspiring and enjoyable. This one was no different. The words were clear and the melody beautiful. He wasn't weak, and he wasn't sick. He left this world in a holy place, before a *Sefer* Torah, praising G-d as he had all of his life.

This book is the story of his life and the life of his helpmate and lifelong companion, my wonderful mother.

PART I – FAMILY HISTORY

MY MOTHER'S STORY

Introduction

MY MOTHER'S STORY should be fairly easy to tell since my children all knew her, at least to some degree. As the family knows, we had the distinct privilege of living next door. Yechiel and Gitti had actually lived with her and the others lived next door and thus interacted with her daily. Even Russi who was only eighteen months old when her Bubbi passed away, has a few precious memories of her. On *Shabbos* afternoons when Russi and I would go next door to visit Bubbi, we would wait for Bubbi to awaken from her nap and come downstairs. When Russi would hear her Bubbi moving around upstairs and knew that she would soon come down, she would check to see if anyone was seated in Bubbi's favorite living room chair. If indeed someone were there, Russi, who was still too young to speak, would pull on that person's legs until he/she got up to make the chair available for her Bubbi. Russi also remembers having certain very special suppers with Bubbi. My mom would sometimes call and ask that I bring "the baby" to have supper with her, I would take Russi next door to Mother's house and leave her there for supper until Mom would call and say, "Chani, we had a really good time, but I'm a little tired now."

It would be appropriate at this point to mention the interaction between Ari and my mom when Ari was about ten. Ari used to enjoy watching TV in Bubbi's house. The one problem was that TV was strictly limited by Bubbi who considered one hour of television at a time to be more than enough. When the program was over, Bubbi would insist that the TV be turned off and would send Ari home with instructions to read a book or to do something else that was constructive. Often, a short time after he had literally been ejected from her house, he would, as he passed by on the porch, knock on the window and with a big smile throw a kiss and call, "Hi Bubbi!" I don't think that Ari could ever have known how much happiness that simple greeting created.

For the purpose of clarification, I have divided the narrative about Mom into the following chapters:

Chapter I: Mom's Siblings

Chapter II: Mom as a Child and Young Adult

Chapter III: Mom Married Dad

Chapter IV: My Mom – Family and Community

Laura Mintz, Aunt Celie, and Toby Ovson

CHAPTER 1
Mom's Siblings

MY MOM had three sisters and three brothers. Aunt Celie, Aunt Lena, Aunt Dena, Uncle Ben, Uncle Joe, and Uncle Simon. My aunts were truly remarkable people; each with a strong and beautiful character. I remember having great love and admiration for each of them, and I would like to share my memories of each one.

The oldest in the family was Aunt Celie (Rivka Tzirel). I can still picture the way she walked, even when she was past sixty: head erect, shoulders back, and spine perfectly straight. She had no patience for those of us who were round shouldered and did not stand up straight. She was very young, about eighteen, when she married Rav Avrohom Yitzchak Ovsovitz and moved to Denver, Colorado and then to Portland, Oregon. She had not borne a child while out West and her husband thought it would be better for them to move back to where the family lived in Philadelphia. It was there that Aunt Celie gave birth to her daughter Deby and her son Jess. There was a severe flu epidemic

Felix, Deby, and Laura　　　　　*Ruth and Bennett Rackman*

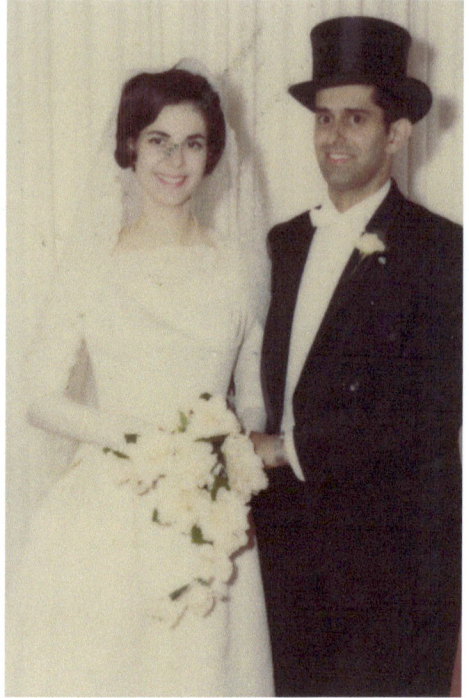

at that time and Rav Avrohom Yitzchok spent much of his time visiting the sick. He undertook the care of an elderly man who was ill with the flu, and as the man recovered, Avrohom Yitzchok caught the flu and died.

Upon the death of her husband, Aunt Celie was left with two little children, Deby, aged four and Jess, aged two. She had to support herself since she had been left no money. Several people, who empathized with her, sent checks, but she sent these checks back and attempted to support herself and her children by opening a small grocery store. Odd though it seems, people who were willing to send her money were not willing to patronize her store, at least not regularly, and so she struggled financially. Since there were no day schools in those days, and since Aunt Celie wanted her children to be both knowledgeable and observant, she hired a *rebbe* to teach them.

Toby and Jess   *Ronnie and Rochelle Adler*

As often as she could, she sent them to Scranton to spend *Shabbos* with their Aunt Laura and Uncle Sam (my parents). It was there that they experienced the Jewish observance that would remain with them throughout their adult years.

Cousin Deby married Felix Taubenblatt, an attorney, and had two daughters: Ruth who married Bennett Rackman and Judy who married Yoseph Tabori. Jess married Toby and had one daughter, Rochelle.

My mom's second sister, Aunt Lena, was married to Uncle Herman Brodie and lived in Philadelphia. Her son Irvin was married to Alene and had three sons: Joey, Steven and Alan Brodie. I remember Aunt Lena as a sweet little lady, soft-spoken and kind, who never really had much of the material things in life, but somehow, it didn't seem to matter, to her that is. It didn't sour her disposition in any way. She was cheerful and giving of whatever she did possess. She had a special

Irvin Brodie   *Alene, Irvin, Uncle Herman, Aunt Lena*

way about her and somehow, she always made us, her nieces and nephews, anxious to be with her. We looked forward to birthdays when she always had something special for us, and among my most prized possessions, I still have a ten karat gold ring with my initials on it which Aunt Lena and Uncle Herman sent me for my tenth birthday.

My mom's third sister, Aunt Dena, was only two years older than my mom. She married a cousin, Uncle Sam Crystal, when she was eighteen years old and moved to Roxbury, Massachusetts, a suburb of Boston where she lived for approximately the first ten or fifteen years of her marriage. Like Mom's other two sisters, Aunt Dena was a truly remarkable person. As Roxbury began to deteriorate, Aunt Dena, Uncle Sam and their three children, Murray, Judy and Sylvia moved to Brookline where they were all very active in the forming of the Young Israel of Brookline and in its activities. Murray married Judy

Aunt Dena and Laura

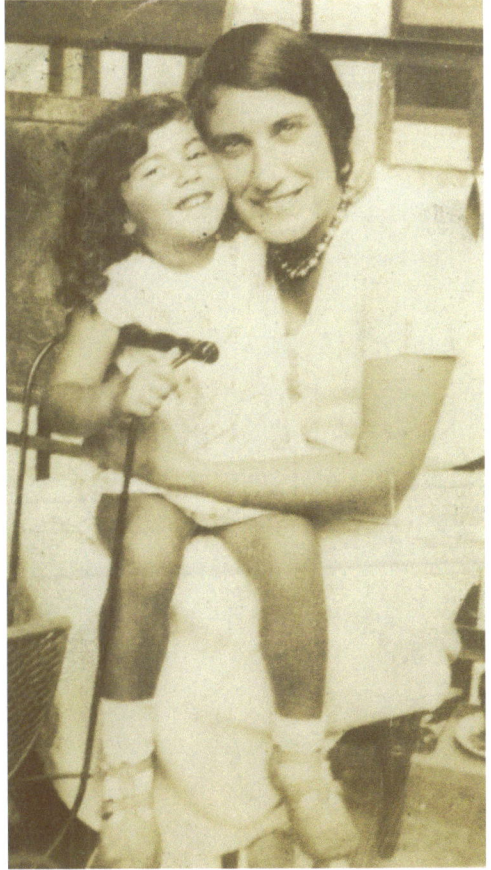

Judy Abromson and Laura

Esther Goldman and had three daughters: Erica, Deby, and Terry; Judy married Bill Abromson and had five daughters: Miriam, Sarah, Deby and twins Ruth and Naomi. Sylvia married Avi Tuchman and had four children: Davida, Syma, Ari and Penina.

Aunt Dena was known and respected by the family and community for her religious observance because she was uncompromising in regards to Jewish law. One example of her observance was her refusal to continue membership with Hadassah when she found out that they would hold their luncheons in non-kosher restaurants. When she confronted the officers of the local chapter with the ultimatum that she would resign her membership unless they changed that policy, she was told that the majority of members were agreeable to sponsoring non-kosher luncheons since they themselves did not keep kosher. Her answer was very definite. "This is not a matter of majority rule. Since Hadassah is a Jewish organization, Jewish law must prevail." When Hadassah refused to comply, Aunt Dena wrote a letter resigning her membership in Hadassah and stating the reason why. Whether it was *kashrus*, *Shabbos*, or family purity, she never would allow for compromise with Jewish law and was very vocal to family and friends about her position. Her unwavering attitude toward religion in her own life gave her a special ability to influence family and friends in Torah observance. My mother was always so proud to visit in Brookline because the Crystal family was the pride of the Orthodox community. Sylvia, with the help of the Bostener Rebbetzin, was responsible for building a *mikvah* in Brookline. This *mikvah* was so significant because before it was built, the women of Brookline had to travel all the way to Roxbury to get to the closest *mikvah*.

An interesting story that Mom use to tell was concerning the birth of Aunt Dena's son Murray. As I mentioned elsewhere in this narrative, my mom's father passed away at age forty-eight. At the time of his death, Aunt Dena who lived in Boston was about ready to give birth to Murray. The family was worried that news of her father's passing might hurt her physically and so they didn't tell her. When Murray was born, Uncle Sam Crystal named him Moshe Isaac after Aunt Dena's father. Since Aunt Dena did not know that her father had passed away, she didn't know what her son's name really was. It became more and more difficult for her husband to tell her the sad news and so he indefinitely postponed doing so. Sometime later when Uncle Sam and Aunt Dena paid a visit to the family in Philadelphia, Aunt Dena referred to her baby by what she thought was his name. An incredulous neighbor who heard her do so, asked why she didn't know that the child was named for her father. We can only imagine the horrible shock for Aunt Dena to have found out about her father's death in this manner. Mom used to say that Aunt Dena never forgave the family for not having told her about her father's death when it happened. Mom said that the family learned an invaluable lesson – that hard as it is to tell sad news, it is important to do so at an appropriate time and place, preferably as soon as possible.

No description of Aunt Dena would be complete without mentioning the package that arrived at our door the day before Shavuoth every year containing Aunt Dena's delicious cheese cake. Now, as my children surely know, I do not like cheese cake, but this cheese cake was different. It consisted of a delicious moist, sweet cinnamon-flavored dough with just a suggestion of cheese. It was the highlight of our *yom tov* – so long ago, but I can still taste it.

Bernie and Morty

As previously mentioned, my mother had three brothers. The oldest, Uncle Ben, lived with his wife, Aunt Anna in Atlantic City. Their five children are: Bernie, Morty, Herbie, Roslyn and Diana. Uncle Ben's sons were in the United States army during the Second World War and all served overseas. Bernie had the especially dangerous job of locating underground mines which had been laid by the Germans in North Africa. My mother said *Tehillim* for all of these nephews for the duration of the war. Unfortunately, I have lost contact

Morty and Betty

Helen and Charles Micklin

with these cousins and have been unable to learn anything about them from members of the family. All I know is that the last name of the men is Kramer and that they live in Atlantic City, New Jersey. The second oldest brother is Uncle Joe, who was married to Aunt Sarah and lived in Philadelphia with his four children: Helen who was married to Charles Micklin; Miriam who was married to Morris Ginsburg; Robert married to Dorothy; and Albert who wasn't married. Aunt Sarah was one of the most cheerful people I have ever known. Her good humor was truly genuine – there was nothing at all phony about it. She concentrated on pleasant things and just seemed not to dwell on the sad or depressing. She wrote often, keeping us up to speed on the news of her family. She would send us things that she had made including bean bags for the children and dresser scarves that she had embroidered (I am still using and enjoying these dresser scarves some thirty years later). I remember that when at one point my mom was ill and in intensive care; Yechiel would visit her during every visiting time – four times a day. He would always read something cheerful to her during these visits, very often a letter from Aunt Sarah. He would joke that he would like to take Aunt Sarah to the West Bank with him because they were in need of people with her upbeat nature and positive attitude.

Miriam, Beverly, Morris Ginsburg

Aunt Sarah spent the last few years of her life in a nursing home in Philadelphia. At that time, our son Dovi drove us to Philadelphia a few times to see her. These visits were treasured by us all since they were the only times that Dovi, Avi, Ari and Russi had the good fortune to get to know Aunt Sarah personally, and to spend some time with her. Russi was about two years old at

Dorothy, Beverly, and Miriam Ginsburg

Albert Kramer

Robert Kramer

Uncle Joe and Aunt Sarah and granddaughters

the time and Aunt Sarah adored her. She was troubled, however, because she wanted to give Russi something and could not think of what to give her. She finally remembered that her Rabbi had given her an aluminum foil menorah, and she was thrilled to be able to give it to Russi, who was equally thrilled to have it. Though it was some time ago, Russi will never forget Aunt Sarah.

Mom's youngest brother was Uncle Simon who lived with Aunt Dora and his children, Fay and Moish Kramer, in Philadelphia. My mom used to go to Philadelphia in August of every year to go to the cemetery (Har Nebo Cemetery where her parents are buried). She would take my siblings and me with her to Philadelphia and leave us at Uncle Simon's house while she was at the cemetery. The great thing about this was that Uncle Simon had a hardware store, and besides the tools, which were fabulous, he carried many toys. To our delight, he literally turned us loose in the hardware store, and designated a place where we were to put all of the things that we wanted. Without fail, on the first

Uncle Simon, Fay, Aunt Dora

day of Chanukah of every year, a huge box arrived from Uncle Simon containing all the things we had picked out and then some, plus a big box of salt water taffy. It was the highlight of our Chanukah. There were toys for everyone plus hammers, nails, screw drivers, pliers, and almost any tool imaginable. I'm sure my siblings feel as I do that to this day when we think of Chanukah, we automatically think of Uncle Simon.

Fay and Sol

Elaine and Moish Kramer

Dr. Moish (Maurice)
Kramer
at his Harvard graduation

Aunt Anna
and Uncle Ben

CHAPTER 2
Mom as a Child and Young Adult

MY MOTHER, whose Hebrew name was Zlata, English name Laura, was born in Riga, Latvia on the fifth night of Chanukah in the year 1899, the seventh of seven children. The name Zlata was after her father's father, whose name was Zavel. Her mother was Tzipporah Gita and her father was Moshe Isaac Kramer, who earned a living as a maker of pots and pans in Riga.

Mom's mother's parents, Chaim Zev and Miriam Crystal, moved from Riga to Jerusalem sometime around 1880, bought a well, and earned their living by selling water. They are both buried in Jerusalem. When my sister lived in Israel in the 1980s she unsuccessfully attempted to locate these graves. Unfortunately, I have been unable to learn anything further about these grandparents.

My mother was only five years old when her parents left Riga, destination Jerusalem. The only remembrance Mother had of Riga was hiding in the basement to escape the *pogroms*[1] especially around Christmas time when the very worst *pogroms* took place. Mom used to say that the Christmas season in Riga was anything but a season of "good will toward men."

On their journey to Jerusalem, Mom's family got as far as the Black Sea, where a flu epidemic prevented them from continuing on to Jerusalem. They went instead to the United States on the ship Ivernia and landed in Boston on September 24, 1906 *(See: Appendix*

---

1. A pogrom is a violent mob attack generally against Jews, and often condoned by the forces of law, characterized by killings and/or destruction of homes and properties, businesses, and religious centers. The term, a Russian word, originally entered the English language to describe 19th and 20th-century attacks on Jews in the Russian Empire; similar attacks against Jews at other times and places also became known as pogroms.

A, Declaration of Intention and Appendix B, Petition for Naturalization).
They settled for a short time in Vineland, New Jersey. The highlight
of that period, as my mother and her siblings would nostalgically recall, was their discovery of fresh tomatoes which they had never seen
in Latvia. In Vineland, tomato plants grew in their backyard, and it
was a thrill to simply pick a tomato off the vine whenever they wanted
to eat one.

The family then moved and settled permanently in Philadelphia
where my grandfather worked as a building contractor until his death
during the flu epidemic of 1922 *(See: Appendix C, Death Certificate of
Moses Kramer).* My mom never said much about her experiences in
the public school system which she attended through secondary
school, but I do remember one particular thing that occurred when
she was eight years old. Mom was very proud of the fact that she had
committed to memory all twenty-two sections of *"The Song of
Hiawatha"* by Henry Wadsworth Longfellow. She was in the third
grade at the time and short for her age. She stood on a chair in the assembly hall and recited by memory all twenty-two sections of the
poem before the entire student body. I am in awe of that accomplish-
ment and cannot even imagine that it is possible for a child of that
age to do so.

Mom had many stories to relate of her two years at Normal
School, the Teachers College in which she attained the degree required
to teach in the public school system in Philadelphia.

My children and grandchildren, and I myself are hard put to
understand how my mom walked to Normal School every day, a
distance of thirty blocks each way, no matter what the weather. What
is most surprising is the fact that she never thought it was a big deal
– as though why not? She often spoke about her non-Jewish and
irreligious Jewish friends who respected her for her consistent and
dedicated commitment to Judaism. Being the only observant Jewish

Laura in Philadelphia

student did not faze my mom or deter her from her proud and complete observance. One of her favorite stories was about her attendance at a luncheon with her fellow student teachers. Since the food was not kosher, Mom brought her own sandwich which she attempted to eat in a manner that would attract the least attention. The college dean, a rather large, elderly woman who was in charge of the program, opened her remarks from the dais by saying, "I see that one person here has taken the liberty to bring her own lunch." All eyes turned toward my mom.

A highlight of my mother's Normal School days was her trip to Bermuda with fellow students. Such a trip in those days was made by boat and necessitated frugality on Mom's part in saving the money to pay for it. It also required careful planning as Mom had to take along her own food, since kosher food could not be bought nor was it available on the boat. My mom had mixed feelings in reminiscing about her trip to Bermuda. Enjoyable thought it was, one could not help but be saddened by the poverty of the natives whose children literally followed carriages begging for pennies. Despite her guide's admonition that throwing coins to the natives would encourage more begging, Mom and her friends felt obligated to give these children as much as they could afford to give them

Sometime after the trip to Bermuda, Mom became ill with pleurisy. Since there were no antibiotics in those days, her life literally hung in the balance for several weeks until the doctors were able to drain the pus and thus promote recovery. During this illness, the name Sarah was added to my mom's name, thus changing the name to Sarah Zlata. It was during her hospitalization at this time that her father passed away. Since Mom was so sick at this time, she was not told of her father's passing until weeks later, after she was discharged from the hospital.

Upon her graduation from Normal School, my mother got a job teaching third grade in the Ludlow School in Philadelphia. She applied for United States citizenship in 1919 and received her citizenship papers in 1923 *(Appendix D, Oath of Allegiance)*. Mom had a favorite story about a trip that she took to a friend's home in Canada during her days as a teacher. Her hostess had decided to serve dinner in the outdoors one evening and set an elegant table on the beautiful grounds outside of her home. Little did she know that there was a beehive nearby. As soon as the food was served, the bees swarmed over the tables forcing each guest to pick up his/ her plate and make a dash for the house. Mom found the situation very amusing and laughed heartily as she ran toward the house. As luck would have it, she opened her mouth wide as she laughed, thereby allowing a bee to fly right into her mouth!

In the years that my mother taught at the Ludlow School, she was the sole support of her mother and herself. Her siblings contributed as much as they could, but since it was during the Great Depression of 1929 and since they had families of their own, they could not help much. In addition to supporting her mother and herself, my mom managed to save enough to pay for her own wedding when she married my father in Philadelphia in 1932. She also saved enough to purchase a lovely walnut seven piece bedroom set which still stands in our home today. Mom's plan, after having married my dad and moved to Scranton was to bring her mother to Scranton to live with her and my dad. That was not meant to be, however, as my Bubba, Tzipporah Gita passed away as the result of a stroke which she suffered three months after Mom's wedding *(See Appendix E, Death Certificate of Zipora Kramer)*.

CHAPTER 3
Mom Married Dad

THE JEWISH COMMUNITY in which my mother found herself in the
Scranton of 1933 was very different from what it is today. There were
six Orthodox Synagogues, three of which were large and beautiful,
and also a *mikvah* in the Flats section of the city. The fact that the
Rav, though a recognized scholar, spoke only Yiddish was the reason
that some community leaders gave for forming a Conservative
Congregation in which an English-speaking Rabbi would function,
and so a large Conservative Temple was formed. There was a sizable
Orthodox community however, and my mom did have friends with
whom she associated. One thing which distinguished her however,
was that my mother wore a *sheitel* which was very unusual in those
days – not only in Scranton, but anywhere. As a general rule at that
time, Orthodox young women did not cover their hair. Aside from a
woman who was considerably older, my mother was the only woman
in town who wore a *sheitel*. There was nowhere to buy a *sheitel* in
Scranton. Before she was married, Mom bought two wigs from a Mr.
Dash who owned a beauty shop in Philadelphia. When she needed a
new *sheitel*, Mom would write and ask Mr. Dash to send her a few
wigs from which to choose. Mom would choose what she wanted and
send the rest back. Buying a wig wasn't the hard part, really. At that
time, if a woman wore a wig it was either because she had lost her hair
or because she had a disease of the scalp. People would point at Mom
as she walked down the street. If she went to buy a hat, invariably she
would see the salespeople huddled in a corner, pointing at her and
laughing. I remember Mom telling me of an instance in which a
Jewish woman actually cornered her while she was grocery shopping
and began scolding: "What kind of a man did you marry anyway that
wants you to be *fahrshtelt*?" (*fahrshtelt* means to masquerade). As was

Laura and Samuel Mintz

her nature, my mom though shaken, responded with resolve and determination, telling whoever was brave enough to confront her, that covering her hair was a religious obligation and furthermore, her own business.

It wasn't until years later that the tide turned and wearing a *sheitel* became the norm as we know it today, not only among Orthodox women but even among non-Jews. Today, one can purchase a wig almost anywhere. We can only ponder what kind of a person our mother was – a young American woman who was educated with, and worked among, non-Jews all her life and had the guts to be different when she knew that she was right.

As mentioned before, my mom was married in December of 1932 when the Great Depression was at its height. My parents lived on the third floor of an apartment house on the 300 block of Penn Avenue, which even in those days was a business district. It was, while living there, that my mom gave birth to my sister Zipora Gita, to me (fourteen months later) and to my brothers – Moshe Aryeh Leib, (eighteen months after me), and Chaim Avrohom two years later – all four of us in five years.

Zipora Gita was named for my mom's mother (a"h) and I Chana Dena, after my mom's Tanta Chana Dena. Mom was so proud to give me that name because her Aunt was a *tzadekes*. In fact, that was how people in her city referred to her. They did not call her by name, but would simply say, "The *Tzadekes*" and everyone would automatically know about whom they spoke.

Laura and Baby Zippy

As is evident, my sister and I were named after members of my mom's family. This was by design because my dad felt that since the mother experiences the pregnancy and the birth, she should have the privilege of choosing the baby's name.

When my brother Moshe was born, Mom intended to name him Moshe Isaac after her father, but she acceded to the request of my zaida (a"h) (my father's father) to give one name after his father whose name was Aryeh. (In the *shtetl* in Europe in which he lived my zaida's father was known as *Leibel Shochet* since he was a *shochet* by trade) Moshe's name is officially Moshe Aryeh Leib.

My brother Chaim Avrohom was named after two people on my father's side. Avrohom is after my dad's brother who passed away at age thirty-six, four months before my brother was born. So as not to give a name after one who died so young, my parents added the name Chaim after my paternal zaida's brother, who was a Torah scholar and who lived to a good old age.

Zipora Gita

Moshe, Laura, Chaim

Even though the Penn Avenue Shul was a mere block away from where we lived and many Jewish people lived in the neighborhood, I don't recall that we ever interacted with other children at that time. (That changed a bit after we moved to the Hill Section, when I was five years old. At that time, the Horowitz family lived around the corner from us and my brothers played with Dovid and Sholom Horowitz.) As was to be the case throughout

Zipora Gita

Chana and Zipora

my childhood, my mother always emphasized that we were fortunate to be siblings who were so close in age and were companions for one another. My mother played with us, sang with us, and taught us every nursery rhyme in existence. We never realized that there was very little money for toys. I remember that our favorite toys were wooden "soldiers" that Mom made from clothes pins. We had a club which literally lasted throughout our young childhood, and since there were four of us, we always had a president, vice-president, secretary and treasurer, on a rotating basis of course. Since there was no day school, we all went to public school. When I was in kindergarten, we moved to a house in the Hill Section on North Webster Avenue. There were trees, grass, flowers, and a big yard – all non-existent on Penn Avenue. This move was at my mom's request since she felt that it was important for us to grow up in surroundings of that kind.

The next decade and a half of my mom's life were concerned with rearing her offspring. Mom always said that during the time in which she was involved in bringing up her children, her only social activity outside the home was PTA because that concerned her children's welfare. We were convinced that Mom could see everything at all times because she said that, since she had been a teacher and since every teacher had eyes in the back of his/her head, that she too had eyes in the back of her head. In those days, children automatically believed what their parents told them and the fact that we did not see eyes in the back of our Mother's head didn't matter. She said that they were there and that was enough reason for us to believe that they were.

Mom's background as a teacher seemed to come in handy in many other ways also. She seemed to have a song, poem, or a story for every occasion. I remember an instance when my third grade teacher told our third grade class that there would be an assembly for Thanksgiving that very af-

Above: Moshe. Below: Chaim.

ternoon at which time each child could either sing a Thanksgiving song or recite an appropriate poem. I came home for lunch bemoaning the fact that I wanted to recite something that was new and different, but did not know what. Mom proceeded to teach me a Thanksgiving song that she had once taught to her third grade class at Ludlow. I did not eat my lunch that day because I sang that song over and over until I knew it well enough to sing it at the assembly that afternoon. As my children are well aware, I too seem to know a song for just about any occasion and I think I can trace that skill right back to my mom. I still remember the second verse to that Thanksgiving song. (I can just hear my children saying, "Please Mom, don't sing that song now.")

Even though I will talk about my dad later in this narrative, I want to digress a bit here to mention my dad's musical ability. He was brought up in a house where there were: a piano, a violin and an accordion. My zaida, a European Jew, loved music and encouraged the children to play, although I do not

Zipora, Laura, Chaim, Moshe

know how many lessons they actually took. My dad used to tell how, as a little boy, he was fascinated with the accordion and could not figure out where the music came from. In order to solve that mystery, he used a scissors to cut the fan part of the accordion in half. I don't think he ever forgave himself for having done that.

My dad too loved to sing and had a beautiful voice. His

zmiros were legendary and literally made the *Shabbosim* and *Yomim Tovim* the magnificent occasions that they were literally the highlights of my childhood. When my dad said a *Haftorah* in shul, it was an occasion that people talked about for a long time. There was a man by the name of Max Bernstein (who will be mentioned later) who would pay $400 every Yom Kippur to buy *Mafter Yonah* for my dad to say. There are people who remember the beauty of that *Haftorah* even today, although my dad is gone some fifty plus years. Dad had a wonderful ear for music as was evidenced in his uncanny ability to pick up a tune when he heard it for the first time. The radio in his place of business constantly played popular music since that is what his employees wanted to hear. Dad had no interest in the lyrics but without even realizing it, he would pick up the melodies and put the words from either *davening* or *Tehillim* to those melodies and would sing them as he worked.

Chani (Chana Dena)

Moshe and Chana

41

CHAPTER 4
Mom – Family and Community

ANY DESCRIPTION of my mother would have to include a reference to her dear friend, Pearl Schorr with whom my mom would speak on a daily basis. I used to have the pleasure of visiting Mrs. Schorr every *Shabbos*, and our conversation often turned to some facet of my mother's life. Among the many things for which Mrs. Schorr admired my mom was for the way she cared for the various members of my father's family over the years. Uncle Abe Rumnianek and Aunt Lilly Rumnianek (neither of whom ever married), who were my father's Uncle and Aunt (my Bubbi Sarah Gittel's brother and sister) lived in our house under my mother's care. But what I remember most was how my mother cared for my zaida until his death when I was twenty-one years old.

The circumstances around which my zaida came to live with us best illustrate who my mother really was. I don't remember Mom ever taking a vacation, and she certainly never went to Florida. At the time to which I refer, Mom had won a Hebrew Day School raffle which entitled her to two weeks for two people in a hotel in Florida. Since my dad could not get away from his business, he suggested that Mom invite one of her sisters to make the trip with her. Mom was packed and ready to go when the call came from my Aunts in New York telling us that they were bringing my zaida to Scranton to live the very next day. Mom did not want to make it seem as though she didn't want to have my dad's father come to live with us, so she never said anything about her Florida plans. She simply unpacked her suitcase and canceled her trip. I took off a semester from college to help with my zaida's care, but basically, the responsibility for his care was my mom's – a job which she discharged with love and devotion as long as my zaida lived.

Uncle Abe Rumnianek,
Rivka and Leibie Puretz

Laura, Aunt Lilly Rumnianek,
Toby Ovson, Ruthie Rackman

It was not until after her offspring were grown and on their own that my mom became involved in community affairs. She was Chairlady of the bake sale at the day school picnic for years and was the first President of the Women's League of the Hebrew Day School. A very important part of her presidency as far as Mom was concerned, was making sure that those families who were not able to contribute financially were nevertheless able to participate in the social functions of the school. An example of this type of concern for others could be illustrated in the following instance. Mom was unsure as to whether a certain family could afford to attend the school's annual *Melave Malka*. She called the family and assured them that their attendance was very important to the success of the affair. She then spoke to the people in charge of admittance and instructed them to make sure that they would "just happen to be absent" from the entrance when the family in question approached so as to save them the embarrassment of being admitted for nothing. This was not an isolated instance but rather the norm in Mom's tenure as President.

My mother's kindnesses were not limited to her activities with the Women's League or with the Shul Sisterhood where she also served as president. Persons who were poor and/or unfortunate seemed to gravitate to Mom and benefited from her kindness. Mrs. Green was a very elderly Jewish widow who lived with Joe, her only son, who was not well. (I will discuss Joe Green in a later part of this narrative.) Mrs. Green would appeal to some Jewish merchants of wholesale dry goods for donations of housedresses, aprons, stockings and scarves and then would sell this merchandise to my mom who would invariably purchase the entire stock, because she reasoned, where else could Mrs. Green sell these things and how would she survive if she did not sell them? Every time this woman appeared at our door, my siblings and I would whisper to one another, "Oh no, not her again," but our Mom would greet Mrs. Green as though she hadn't seen her for a long time and was really in need of whatever it was that she had for sale at that time.

Another friend of my mom was Rose Schiff, a single lady who worked in a department store in Scranton for many years. She belonged to our Shul but did not attend services except for the High Holidays. Rose lived with her mother all her life and had no friends at all except for my mom whom she called regularly to complain about her sad lot in life. She was lonely and constantly quarreled with her mother who was both bossy and overprotective. She was very hard hit at her mother's death, however, especially since she experienced guilt at having been unappreciative and really downright nasty to her mother during all their years together. My mom comforted Rose by assuring her that her mother had loved her unconditionally and that she could best honor her mother's memory by remembering all of the good times that they spent together of which there must have been many.

Epilogue

"My Mother's Story" would be in no way complete without the thoughts of some family members, besides myself, who loved and admired her. Some memories of her children and grandchildren were verbally expressed at our First Annual Mintz Family Reunion, which was held at Beth Shalom Synagogue in Scranton in the summer of 2004.

My brother, Moish, recalled an incident that happened to Mom a few years after he and my brother Chaim had left home to study at Ner Israel Yeshiva. Mom was walking home from town one afternoon and stopped at the intersection of Jefferson Avenue and Linden Street to wait for traffic to pass. A truck loaded with wood approached and Mom instinctively stepped back quickly. As the truck passed her, several large pieces of wood fell off, landing in the exact spot where she had been standing an instant before. It wasn't until a bit later when she had reached home and had had a chance to reflect on what had happened that she realized how close she had come to serious injury or perhaps even worse. She returned to that intersection and spoke to the policeman who was there and had witnessed her near accident. Mom told him that she was sure she had been saved because she had two sons who were studying in a Rabbinical Seminary.

Yechiel Leiter, who was the oldest grandson present at the reunion, and probably had spent more time with his Bubbi than any of the others besides for Gitti, had some interesting stories to tell. He recalled how Bubbi's preparations for *Shabbos* began early Friday morning when as a toddler he assisted her in the chopping of fish for gefilte fish. He recalled the time he had turned the bowl of fish over onto the floor in a split second when Bubbi had turned around to get something. He told how in later years when he was in the Israeli army, Bubbi had written letters of encouragement to him. He said that he had passed the letters around to his fellow soldiers who could not believe that a grandmother would write: "It is the call of the hour, Yechiel. You have the honor to help defend the people of Israel in the land of Israel. Go forward: do the job to the best of your ability; and may Hashem crown your efforts with success." Yechiel recalled that his Bubbi's letters served regularly as an inspiration to him as well as to the rest of the soldiers in his unit whose letters from their grandmothers usually went something like this: "Be careful. Try not to get hurt, and maybe, just maybe, you can get someone else to go in your place!"

Phil Hymowitz told of advice that Bubbi had once given him which helped him in his childhood and throughout his adult life. "If you are ever afraid of anything," Bubbi would advise, "say *Adon Olam* and your fears will go away." Phil said he had followed this advice many times but found it especially helpful when he served in the Israeli army and found himself in situations fraught with dangers. Phil recalled how Bubbi kept in touch with each grandchild and made it her business to know each one well, and was concerned to know where he/she was and what he/she was doing.

This sentiment was echoed by Hayim Leiter who recalled how Bubbi would sit down with him each time he came home from the Yeshiva and would want him to give her a detailed account of how things were going in school. Hayim also told us how *Tisha B'Av* has always been a most meaningful day to him because when Bubbi read from the *Tzene V'rena* about the destruction of the *Beis Hamikdash*, she cried as though she had actually experienced it herself. It was a very personal thing to her – not a historical event that had happened long ago to someone else.

Gitti Leiter Horowitz had actually lived with Bubbi, and besides for her brother Yechiel, had spent more time with her than anyone else that was present. Gitti told us how careful Bubbi was with what she ate. Her favorite lunch in the summertime was a cut-up peach and banana with a scoop of sour cream on it, and a glass of cold milk. As she drank the milk, she would say very enthusiastically: "This is so refreshing, so delicious!" If offered a piece of chocolate, Bubbi was wont to say, "That chocolate looks delicious and I will have a piece tomorrow, I have already had my chocolate for today." She would then produce a bar of chocolate from which one square was missing. Though Bubbi really enjoyed her chocolate, she never ate more than one square a day.

Gitti also recalled a night when she and Bubbi, who were asleep in a second floor bedroom, were awakened suddenly by a loud noise in the kitchen downstairs. Gitti, who was in a very agitated state, phoned me next door demanding that I do something immediately. I awakened Avi and Dovi, who armed themselves with helmets and baseball bats and went next door to Bubbi's house. As they entered with their bats in the air, they met Bubbi coming down the stairs to see what had happened. As it turned out, the noise was the crash of pots and pans that had been piled high atop one another on the dish rack. Bubbi had to reassure Gitti that there was no danger so that she would come out from under her bed, where, in her fright, she had sought refuge.

Some of the other grandchildren who were present recounted special memories which they had of Bubbi. Eliyahu Mintz said that he had thought that Bubbi must be very rich because she always sent a crisp new ten-dollar bill on his birthday. Dassy Brown recalled Bubbi's letters in which the ten-dollar bill was enclosed. She said that she has kept these letters all these years because the handwriting is so beautiful and they are all signed with "XXXXX" (kisses). Dassy also recalled how Bubbi would say, *"Shlof gesundt: shate-uf gezunterkeit,"* as she wished her grandchildren "Good night." Dassy said that she continues that tradition with her own children.

Dov Leiter mentioned Bubbi's calmness during exciting and/or potentially dangerous times. He told of an incident which occurred late one night when he had been cooking something in Bubbi's house. Whatever was cooking burned, and set off the smoke alarm. Bubbi just called down from upstairs to make sure that he was aware of the situation. She was not upset; did not scold; nor did she even inquire as to how he was dealing with the problem. She just trusted him to take care of things by himself.

Avi Leiter also told of Bubbi's calm and pleasant disposition. He said that in all of his adult life, he has never met anyone who was like her, because she never said a negative word about anyone. He recalled that Bubbi's reaction to a family discussion that turned negative about someone was to very unobtrusively leave the room.

Ari Leiter spoke of Bubbi's love of peace and her desire that she and her children pursue it by dwelling on the things on which they agree, and minimizing, or better yet, eliminating discussion on things of which they disagree. She valued peace among family members as the one thing she prized among all else, and she prayed that her children and grandchildren would never allow dissension in any form to exist among them. Ari said that he has many times throughout his adult life seen the wisdom of Bubbi's admonition to actively pursue peace. He noted that he has observed the bitterness in some families where some family members allow disagreements which are often minor, unimportant, and inconsequential to cause serious rifts among family members. Ari considered Bubbi's love of peace and her exhortation for her family to pursue it, to be her major legacy. Ari concluded his memories of his Bubbi on an amusing note. He recalled how he always knew when Bubbi was at the door when she came to have supper with us on Friday nights. Instead of knocking, she would rattle her keys against the door window. It was her unique way of letting us know that she had arrived and wanted to come in.

MY FATHER'S STORY
CHAPTER I
Dad's Family and Early Childhood

MY BUBBI, Sarah Gittel Rumnianek, my dad's mother, was born and grew up in Prushnitz, a *shtetl* in Poland. According to information that I received from the National Archives and Record Administration *(See Appendix F)* in Pittsfield, Massachusetts, Bubbi was born in January of 1874. Bubbi Sarah Gittel never attended school, but taught herself to read and write Yiddish and Hebrew; she made no attempt to learn English.

Bubbi Sarah

I'm not sure why, but I think it was probably because she did not want to become in any way integrated into American society. She thought that learning the language was the first step toward that end. My brother Chaim recalled that our Bubbi, Sarah Gittel, would refer to English as a *modenah shprach* – an odd language, citing as examples the words, "room, broom, and bedroom" which struck her as amusing.

Bubbi's parents were Esther Rannah and Zalman Dov Rumnianek. She had one brother, Avrohom Henoch *(Uncle Abe; See Appendix G, Ellis Island Foundations)*, and two sisters: Leah Nicha (Aunt Lily), and Chana Ruchel. Zalman Dov Rumnianek passed away at a relatively young age leaving his widow with four small children. Poverty was rampant among Polish people in general, and among Jews in particular. Esther Rannah was in an especially bad financial bind because she had no provider for a number of years until Avrohom Henoch (who was known in the family as Uncle Abe) became old enough to learn the trade of tailoring and earned a livelihood as a tailor for the Russian Army. I really don't know how she managed to eke out an existence for herself and her family. Uncle Abe, who never married and lived with my family, used to regale us with stories of his childhood. One thing that stood out in his memory was how his mother would put her infants to sleep when she ran short of milk. She would put a few drops of *schnaps* (whiskey) on the babies' lips in order to lull them to sleep. Our Bubbi Esther Rannah would make sure to cook something with an appetizing odor so that people passing by the house would not think she was lacking for food; she did not want charity.

Other stories that Uncle Abe would tell, concerned the rabid anti-Semitism in Prushnitz and in Yaaneveh, where they also lived during their childhood years. He recalled being ambushed and hit in the head with stones as he came home from *cheder* each day, and was forced on a regular basis to detour to the home of the *felsher* who was the equivalent of a physician's assistant, meaning, he wasn't an M.D. but did have some medical training. The *felsher* bandaged Uncle Abe's head so that he could continue on his way home with minimal pain.

In his adult years, Uncle Abe became an excellent tailor, a perfectionist in his trade, so that he was good enough to be a tailor in the Russian Army, where he made uniforms for the soldiers. These uniforms had to be perfect down to the last detail, or else! The Russian Army did not deal kindly with those who made mistakes.

Uncle Abe came to the United States in 1903. He departed from the port of Bremen aboard the Friedrich der Grosse, arriving at Ellis

Island on August 26 *(See Appendix G, Passenger Record)*. He had many stories to tell of the misery which he, and so many like him, had endured on their trip to America. The fact that they had so little money forced them to get the cheapest accommodations on the bottom of the boat. They suffered terrible seasickness for the duration of the trip, but they didn't dare admit to being sick at all, because they were afraid that sickness would cause them to be sent back. So they suffered in silence.

When Uncle Abe arrived in the United States, he had no money and so he sold eggs door to door for a while in order to accumulate enough money to set up a tailor shop. One of his favorite stories about his experiences in the egg business concerned the time when a prospective customer invited him into her house to wait while she served lunch. Uncle Abe was very impressed with the spacious home, especially the dining room where a lovely table was set with an Irish linen table cloth, beautiful china, and crystal goblets. When she was ready to serve, the woman called out, "Jack, come in. I'm ready to serve lunch." In came a huge dog and climbed up on a chair at the table. Uncle Abe would chuckle as he recounted this story and say, "I can see that it is better to be a dog in America than a Jew in Russia!"

Uncle Abe eventually settled in Scranton. He lived with us, and opened his own tailor shop where he was known as the "Jefferson tailor." As previously mentioned, he was a perfectionist at sewing and did all of the sewing in the house. He made my dad's wedding suit, which was equivalent of a tuxedo at the time – striped trousers and a cutaway jacket. That suit is in the cedar drawer of the chest-on-chest in the master bedroom at 302 Madison. Uncle Abe also made several beautiful suits for my mom. He knew the whole *Tehillim* by heart and would recite it all every day as he sat sewing.

Upon their arrival in the United States, his sister Chana Ruchel settled in Birmingham, Alabama. I'm not sure why, but I think it was probably because she married someone who settled there. We lost track of her since, as far as I know, she never paid us a visit, and I don't think we even knew her married name. Leah Nicha (known to us as Aunt Lily) never married, and settled in New York where she made her home with married nieces and/or nephews. I knew her quite well, however, because she often came to visit in Scranton during my childhood.

My Zaida, Shraga Feivel Mintz, my dad's father, was born in M'lave, Poland, around 1875 *(See Appendix F, National Archive and Records)*. His father's name was Aryeh

Zaida Shraga

Leib, and since he was a *shochet*, the people of the town referred to him as a "*Leibele shochet*". I have been unable to learn my Zaida's mother's name. My Zaida did have siblings, but since all fell victims to the Holocaust, my Zaida never spoke of them and so I know literally nothing about them. I do know that he had a brother named Chaim who was a Torah scholar and lived to a good old age; my brother Chaim was named for him. Zaida Shraga Feivel lived in M'lave, or Warsaw, (I am not sure how long he lived in M'lave, the city of his birth) until the early 1890s when he was scheduled to be drafted into the Russian Army. This presented a major dilemma as the Russian army made it all but impossible for a Jew to remain religious. He posed the question of what he should do to the *Tzfas Emeth*, who was the *Gerrer Rebbe* at that time, and he advised him to go to the United States, with the admonition: "If you will keep the Torah then the Torah will keep you."

According to the Passenger Record *(See Appendix H, Ellis Island Foundation, Passenger Arrivals)*, my Zaida was in Prushnitz before boarding to come to America. We can conclude that he went there to meet Bubbi Sarah Gittel since that was where she lived. We can only speculate why they

Shraga Feivel, Sarah Gittel, Mordechai Yaakov (Max)

didn't marry there and make the journey to America together. Zaida boarded the ship Rhynland in Antwerp and arrived at Ellis Island on January 2nd 1892 *(and see Appendices H and I Ellis Island Foundation)*.

He was married to my Bubbi Sarah Gittel in Boston in 1895 *(See Appendix F, Marriage Register of Shraga Feivel Mintz and Sarah Gittel Rumnianek)*. They settled in Boston where Zaida worked as a *schochet*. My dad, Zalman Dov (Samuel B.), who was the *b'chor* (the first born son), was born on August 30th 1896 *(See Appendix J, Birth Certificate of Samuel Mintz)*; the second child, Mordechai Yaakov (Max J.), was born in 1898 *(See Appendix F)*. My Zaida's boss pressured him to modernize his appearance by trimming his beard. Zaida responded by leaving Boston and moving his family to Bath, Maine, where he was the *schochet* for that city and several nearby ones as well. While in Bath, Bubbi Sarah Gittel gave birth to three more sons and one daughter. They were: Moshe *(Mose, See Appendix F)*; Malka (Mollie); Avrohom (Abraham, nicknamed Bummi); and Yosef Binyamin (Joseph B., nicknamed Yossel).

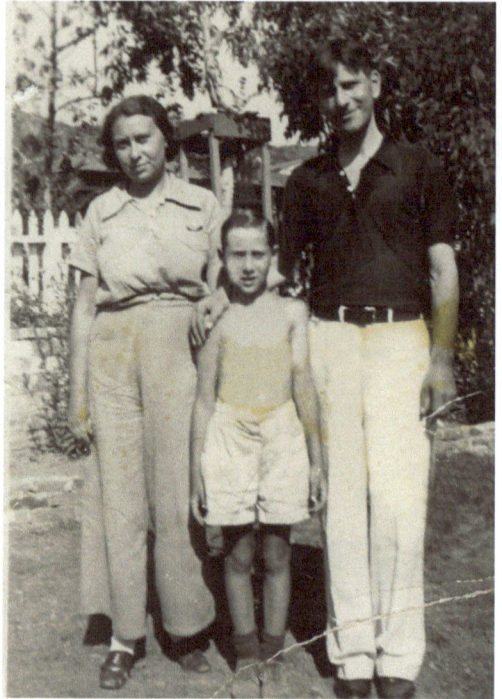

Moshe   *Mollie, Charles, Bummi*

Dad loved to regale us with stories of his childhood in Bath. Though a young child, he was very much involved in "business pursuits" in order to earn the money that he wanted to have, since he did not look to his parents for anything besides food, clothing and shelter, none of which were in abundance at any time. When he was five years old, he earned money by cleaning out the spittoons that were in many of the offices and businesses at that time. Such a job would probably not appeal to most people, especially not to children. It was, however, in keeping with the philosophy which my dad would espouse all of his life. He would exhort us, "Do not worry about the dirt that you get on yourself that you can wash off, worry about the dirt on your *neshama* (soul). Be very careful of your actions, because improper actions are the "dirt on the soul" and that kind of dirt cannot be washed off."

Since Bath was a port, it afforded our Dad a very unique way of earning money. Many large ships would dock on the coast, but could not come in close to the shoreline. Sailors had a lot of money, but no place to spend it, since they could not leave the ship even to buy a newspaper. Between the ages of ten and twelve, Dad would rent a row-boat and row out to the ships to sell newspapers. The papers cost him something like two cents apiece, and he sold them for a dollar.

Other pursuits afforded Dad and his brothers the opportunity to enjoy things most children take for granted. Dad knew how to run a movie projector and would regularly show the movies at the local theater so that he and his siblings saw them with no charge. Dad also organized a group of his brothers and their friends to put up posters around town advertising the movie being shown that week. He would assemble all of his helpers who would be given free tickets to the show as a reward for their work. The circus, which was an annual event in Bath, was an experience

Chani and Yossel

to which Dad and his siblings looked very much forward. On the morning of the show, they were up at four AM and on the grounds at five to help put up the circus tents. In payment for their work in this regard they were given tickets to the show.

Dad never tired telling us of the tremendous patience his father exhibited in imparting to his children his love for Jewish learning and observance. I think his all-time favorite was the *Shabbos* afternoon story his father would tell him and his brothers. Each week, his father would assemble his three oldest sons in his bedroom when he would lie down after *Shabbos* lunch, to tell them about the *Parsha* of the week. In the summer, the windows were open, and, as their father talked to them, they were focused on the sounds of the baseball game taking place on the street below. The cries of "Strike one, strike two, etc." reminded them on an ongoing basis that the ballgame was in progress, and that they were missing it. Eventually their father fell asleep, whereupon they climbed out of the second story window, slid down the rain pipe, and happily joined their beloved ballgames. Every week their father summoned them to hear the *Parsha* and each time, as soon as he fell asleep, they slid down the rain pipe to join the game. That is, they did this until it occurred to them one day, that their father never tired of telling them of the *Parsha* because it was so important to him. The ballgame suddenly lost its importance, and they no longer had the desire to become a part of it. They had learned the true meaning of *Shabbos* by mere observation of their father. It was a lesson that our Dad passed onto his offspring as will be explained in a later chapter.

Another story that Dad used to tell, as he chuckled in remembrance, was about the Fourth of July, a day to which Dad and his brothers looked forward with great anticipation. There were no laws regulating fireworks at that time, and the Fourth was very dangerous since fireworks such as Roman Candles often caused serious injury. Bubbi Sarah Gittel knew that her children were anxious to have firecrackers for the Fourth and that they would find a way to buy them. She sought to solve the problem by taking away their shoes and socks, and she suggested that they play in the house. Not ready to give up their Fourth of July celebration so quickly, they went out barefoot to see what they could do to find some firecrackers. When the local policeman was told of their plight, he gave them a crisp new five-dollar bill with the instruction to buy as many firecrackers as they could. You can imagine Bubbi Sarah Gittel's reaction when she found out how the boys got the firecrackers. Dad used to say that he never heard his mother call anyone else the names that she called the policeman that day.

Dad would tell us about the tremendous snowstorms in Bath and how cold it was there. Their house was heated by a coal stove and the fire had to stay lit for the house to remain warm. *Shabbos* was especially difficult since, if the fire went out it could not be relit, and the house would become freezing cold. This happened one *Shabbos*; Bubbi Sarah Gittel went out to find a non-Jew to light the coal stove, so that the children would not be cold. She stood in waist-high snow, in the freezing cold, until she found a man who agreed to come to the house to light the stove. When they got to the house, the man suddenly decided that there must be something peculiar going on in that house where people wanted a stranger to light the coal stove. He turned and ran, leaving Bubbi Sarah Gittel with no one to light the stove, and with six unhappy children.

As previously mentioned, Dad started to work at a very young age. His work was not just for things which he wanted, like movies and the circus, he was the oldest and his parents depended on his help in providing for the family. One thing that he had to do was to drive the horse and wagon. I am not quite sure exactly why they needed a horse and wagon; but I was told that it was important. On one occasion my Zaida took Dad, who was eight years old at the time, with him when he went to purchase a horse. When the owner of the horse, an elderly Greek man, realized that the horse was going to be driven by a little boy, he exclaimed in his thick Greek accent: "She is a wild horse!" Zaida's answer was: "My son is a strong boy." Dad did not contradict his father, (since no child would have thought to do that at that time), but he was terribly frightened. Zaida bought the horse because the price was right, but Dad recalled how he had to drive the wagon pulled by that wild horse. The year was about 1905 and there were a few Model T's on the road. When the horse came near a car, she became frightened and reared up. Dad had to hold onto the reins with all his might to keep the horse from running away. That experience followed him all of his life.

When my dad was twelve, and Uncle Yossel was one year old, the family moved to Scranton. The reason for the move from Bath was that my grandparents did not want to bring up their children in a place where there were no other religious Jews. Financially, it was a tremendous step-down since Scranton did not need another *shochet* and Zaida therefore had no way of earning a living. The family settled briefly in Old Forge, but then moved to Raymond Court in Scranton, where Zaida opened a butcher shop. He did not have the temperament to deal with the customers, and so our Dad, who was just post Bar Mitzvah, left school in order to run the store.

CHAPTER 2
The Move to Scranton

DAD MARKED his Bar Mitzvah in Scranton about a year after the family moved there from Bath, Maine. Actually, the only memory he recounted about the Bar Mitzvah was when his father took him to buy a suit in a second hand store. Dad, who as an adult, never wanted to wear something that had been worn by someone else, was even at that time not feeling good about shopping in that store in the first place.

To add insult to injury, his father did not want to pay five dollars for the suit that they chose and told Dad that they could no doubt do better somewhere else. I don't think that Dad ever really forgot how disappointed he was that day. Even though five dollars in 1909 was a sizeable sum for a suit, it seemed like a reasonable amount to my dad, who was not inclined to look for something cheaper. I should emphasize here that Dad certainly did not communicate his disappointment to his father, since children in those days did not voice disapproval of what their parents said or did. I think, however, that it did make a lasting impression on him. Even later on, when money was no longer a problem for him, he never bought any article of clothing or anything else for that matter which was not new and good quality.

As mentioned previously, my zaida was not allowed to *shecht* in Scranton and so he opened a butcher shop at 441 Penn Avenue. The family at first lived in a second floor apartment on Raymond Court. Dad used to reminisce about the fact that they were very much isolated since they had no Jewish neighbors. It didn't seem to matter however. He had very happy memories of *Shabbos* and Yom Tov meals with the family, singing and learning together. Money was scarce, but that did not seem to matter either. As the oldest son, Dad left school after 8th grade in order to help run the store. One of his duties was to deliver orders, so he needed a car. The only car on the lot that he could afford was a Model T that didn't seem in such good shape, but my dad thought it would serve his purpose, and besides it was the only one that he could afford. I remember the rest of the story with some pain because Dad always teared up when he told it. After he had paid for the car and was driving out of the lot, the roof of the car blew off. My dad drove that car without a roof for some time after that as the snow and the rain came down on him, until he could afford to buy another car. He would recount how he endured the laughter and jeering of people who thought that the sight of someone driving such a car was funny. Dad admitted being hurt, but would comfort himself with the fact that he had paid for it and did not owe anybody anything.

When he was fourteen, my dad happened to meet a gentleman who owned a hide cellar. I can recall that he said to himself the first time he met the man and actually saw the hide cellar, "Does society really expect a person to make a living in a place like this? The smell is terrible!" He would smile as he then exclaimed, "Two weeks later, I owned the place." The owner had become sick and offered to sell the business to my fourteen-year-old Dad for the four hundred dollars which he had managed to save in the bank. His mother had to go with him to the bank to withdraw the money since he was too young to do so by himself. He ran the business very successfully for the next five years, and through hard work and efficient management was well on his way towards becoming a successful entrepreneur.

It was at this point that my Bubbi, Sarah Gittel, intervened and insisted that Dad leave the business and go to the Yeshiva in New York. She could not accept the fact that any of her sons would grow up without a yeshiva education, and so to please his mother, my dad went to Yeshivah Rabbeinu Yitzchack Elechonan for the next four years. He often recounted that he had money in the bank and his check book with him, and could have gone to a Broadway show, or anywhere else he wanted to go for that matter, but he never did. At first he was very lonesome for Scranton in general and for his home in particular. The Yeshiva did not serve meals in those days and the students had to eat in a restaurant. Dad used to say that when he made *Kiddush* for the first time in the restaurant, he was so terribly homesick that he remembered thinking, "If the world doesn't come to an end right now, it never will." He would tell us that even if he didn't particularly feel like learning one day, when he approached the *Bais Medrash* and heard the enthusiastic learning that was in progress, he became enthused to join in.

Dad never liked New York; in fact he disliked it intensely. It was so busy, so impersonal, with people so absorbed with their own pursuits that they seemed to have no time to even notice those around them. One thing that made a particular impression on him, was the poverty of the Jews who lived in the neighborhood of the Yeshiva on the East Side of New York. Most lived on the third and fourth floors of the tenement houses, and most had no iceboxes in which to keep perishable food. (Refrigerators were uncommon or even nonexistent in most homes in those days.) These people kept their food out on the fire escape which was the most reasonable place, in fact the only place possible, for them to keep the food. The problem was that it was against fire regulations to keep anything on the fire escape, and fire inspectors who made periodic inspections of the property would simply knock the food off the fire escape and onto the ground below. This anti-Semitic disregard for these poor people who had no alternative place to keep their food and did not have the means to replace it, angered my dad and upset him even when he recounted the incident years later.

As previously stated, my dad was in the Yeshiva for four years, until about age 23. It was a short time relatively speaking, but his devotion to learning and his ability to make maximum use of his time enabled him to amass more knowledge than normal and develop a love for learning that would be with him all his life.

CHAPTER 3
Beginning Business

WHEN MY DAD left the Yeshiva and returned to Scranton, he decided that it was a good time to embark on a new business. The hide business involved very hard work and an unpleasant odor. So Dad felt that, while still a young man, he wanted to try another business. He found a business which manufactured shovels and decided to buy that. The purchase involved his own money as well as money borrowed from others. Dad really didn't know anything about the actual manufacture of the shovels, so he retained the workers who had worked in the factory before and would continue under the direction of a foreman who had experience as well. Dad would go on the road and do the selling. He was a good salesman and his sales steadily increased.

The problem was production, which lagged further and further behind. Dad was puzzled about this until one Friday when fate helped him solve the mystery. His Model T needed some repair, and so he decided to go back to Scranton a few hours earlier than usual. Arriving at the factory unexpectedly early, he found the foreman and workers busily engaged in a game of cards. Needless to say, the reason for the decreased production became clearly evident. The foreman and workers had decided that since the boss really had no experience in the actual production of the shovels, he would not know how many shovels should be produced in a day, and so they set the schedule for production. Dad realized his mistake in attempting to run a business in which he had no experience. He dealt with the problem very quickly and decisively, telling the workers that the factory was shut down. He said, "I just put a lock on the door and left." Of course much of the money that he lost when he closed the business was money that he had borrowed, and which he was obligated to pay back. He assured all to whom he owed the money that he would pay it back no matter how long it took. He used to tell us that he would never avoid these people during the entire time it took him to pay them back. He would go out of his way to face them, and assure them that he was working on it and that he would pay them back as soon as he possibly could. Dad could have, and some would say should have, declared bankruptcy, but he did not. It took him eleven difficult and long years, but he did pay back every penny that he owed. He would tell us with tears in his eyes, how he had worked day and night to earn the money to repay what he had borrowed. "Many nights I just lay down on the cold marble counter in my store and didn't even take the shoes off my feet as I caught a few hours sleep before I went back to work."

Not owing anybody any money was one of the principles by which my dad lived all his life. He postponed getting married until he had made back all that he had lost in the shovel business. That took until 1932, at which time Dad met and married my mother in December of that year.

CHAPTER 4
Dad and His Siblings

To COMPLETE "My Dad's Story", I need to describe his relationship with his siblings. As mentioned previously, Dad was the firstborn son (the *b'chor*) and as such played an important role in supporting the family. He left formal schooling for full-time work after his Bar Mitzvah and owned his own business by age 14. His earnings enabled his sister and brothers to finish high school and his brothers to study full-time in Yeshivas. Dad had a deep love of his siblings and was proud to play a major role in their education. He himself loved learning and spent every spare moment reading or studying. Though his formal education was limited to four years in the yeshiva (between ages 19–23) he was self-educated in both Torah and secular studies. He was proud of the educational and professional accomplishments of his siblings and often touted their achievements. Abraham (Bummie) was a graduate of Rush Medical School, the University of Chicago, and practiced medicine in Newark, New Jersey. Joseph B. (Uncle Yossel), received *smicha* from Yeshiva Torah v'Da'ath. Dad was so proud to tell of how the *rabbaim* who tested Uncle Yossel for *smicha* said that had Uncle Yossel taken the *bechina* one hundred years previous in Europe, he would have been considered an outstanding scholar.

What most impressed me concerning my dad and his siblings, was his relationship with brother Max. Uncle Max was the second born of the siblings, about two years younger than Dad. He was a brilliant student and a gifted speaker, even in his teenage years. He graduated from Technical High School in Scranton, where he was chosen to give the reply to the Mantle Oration in his Junior year, and the Mantle Oration at his graduation one year later. It should be noted that the Mantle Oration was awarded to the student who was judged the best speaker among the many who auditioned. Uncle Max went on to study at Yeshiva

Rabbenu Yitzchok Elchanan where he received *smicha*. He had the distinction of being one of the first two American-born men to attend a yeshiva in America. He was a pulpit rabbi for many years, most of the time in Brooklyn, New York at the Talmud Torah of Flatbush.

The relationship between Dad and Uncle Max was so special because of the deep respect and admiration they had for each other. As long as I can remember, they worked as a team in helping to solve any family problems and/or difficulties. When their mother became ill, Uncle Max took charge of her daily care, both in his home in Flatbush and during her hospitalizations. He dealt with the doctors and nurses and saw to it that her every need was met. He was her constant companion and set aside a period each day when they said *Tehillim* together. Since Dad was in Scranton at that time, his share for the care for his mother was financial; he paid the bills. What I admired most was the way the brothers talked on a regular basis and planned for their mother's care, and the role that each would take. This was their modus operandi, the way they dealt with family problems and/or the difficulties with which they were presented. My dad was proud of Uncle Max and this feeling was mutual.

Actually, my dad's attitude in this regard was a particular source of wonder for me. The difference in age between Uncle Max and Dad was only about two years. Dad could have legitimately requested that they share the responsibility of family support as they were growing up so that each one could have had access to equal educational opportunities. Dad was willing to forego his formal education in favor of his brother, and he was always happy to have done so. He was so proud of his brother's accomplishments. As for Uncle Max he was equally proud and admiring of Dad and revered him for the kind of person that he knew Dad to be. In the section of this narrative which deals with transcriptions (Section III), there's a speech that was given by Uncle Max at Dov's Bar Mitzvah. It is in this speech that Uncle Max describes

Dad in his own words, and explains to Dov how blessed he is to have been given his grandfather's name.

PART II – MEMOIRS

Chapter i

Dad in Business

As we grew up, my siblings and I were constantly presented with the fact that our dad was special. Our mother would remind us often that our Dad was "one in a million", and we knew that since she lived with him she should know. My siblings and I always felt special because whenever we would mention our name, the response we got was an incredulous, "You're Sam Mintz's children!" Of course we didn't really need the praise of others to feel special, because our parents made us feel that way all of the time. I am sure that the phrase that we heard most often growing up, was, "You are such smart children, what do you think about that?" in regard to whatever was being discussed at the time.

As mentioned previously, our Dad's business was curing hides and skins, which he purchased from the local slaughter houses and sold to tanneries in New England. His kosher meat market was open only on Thursdays. Dad employed several workers, but he worked with them besides doing the selling and bookkeeping. His business hours were from around 6am to somewhere around 8pm. Needless to say, we did not see much of our Dad at home during the week. But he was always as near as the phone and we were with him to help whenever possible; Mother to take phone calls, and we children, to take the chickens to be *schechted* and to pluck them. My brothers worked in the hide house. Even when they went to the Yeshiva, they continued to work during vacation time. They proved to be of invaluable assistance, especially on a *motzei Shabbos* or a *motzei yom tov* when they often worked through the night.

Spending time in our Dad's business afforded us a first opportunity to see him in action. His philosophy in running his business was the same as his philosophy of life. Money was a necessity, a medium of exchange. A man is obligated to support his family, but Dad's philosophy could be summed up in the simple phrase, "It is good when you have money, not when money has you." This was not just a saying for him, it was a way of life, which we as children saw him demonstrate in business transactions every day. There was one occasion in which Dad realized that the scale in his butcher shop had malfunctioned, resulting in several overcharges for customers on that particular day. Difficult though it was, Dad took the time to review each sale, in order to determine exactly how much he had overcharged each customer. He notified the customers of the error and repaid every one.

At least six men a day (*meshulochim*) came to our place of business to collect for yeshivas or for the poor and needy. My dad would request that each one would tell him a *dvar torah* before receiving a sizable donation. When Mom questioned the feasibility of handing out so much money, Dad would say that he got much more from them than they got from him.

In addition to contributions to individuals, Dad regularly lent sizable amounts to Jewish businessmen as well as to Ner Israel and other yeshivas which would borrow at the beginning of the month and pay back at the middle of the month. People were thus able to meet their payrolls, and yeshivas to meet their expenses and pay teachers. Unfortunately, there were those who did not repay the loans. If my dad got a check that he thought might not be good, he did not deposit it, because he said it would be a *chillul Hashem* (a desecration of G-d's name) for the bank to see that a Jew had written a bad check.

It would be impossible for me to even attempt to enumerate how many people Dad helped. He believed that it was not possible to do too much for any Jew, because a Jew is special. He/she has a *neshama* (a soul) which is a *chelek Eloha mema'al* (I'm not going to translate that). People would tell us that we had no idea how many people in the community our Dad had either set up or kept in business. However I would like to mention a few.

Mr. Jerry Ganz, newly married, came to Scranton to start a construction business. Dad loaned him money so that he could enter a carpentry contest in which he could possibly win a sizable sum which he very much needed to start his business. Upon receiving the money, Mr. Ganz made a verbal commitment to pay it back. He then asked if Dad would like him to put the commitment in writing. Dad's reply was one Mr. Ganz never forgot. "Mr. Ganz, if your word means nothing then your paper also means nothing."

Max Bernstein was a Jew who at a young age had been abandoned by his father, and was brought up in a non-Jewish orphanage. He grew into adulthood with neither a Jewish nor a secular education. As a young man, he began to gamble and developed a very bad business reputation. As a result, he was unable to secure the financial assistance necessary to start a business. Dad promised to help "Maxi" if he would agree to stop gambling. Having exacted this promise, Dad accompanied "Maxi" to the bank for the purpose of "securing a business loan for Max Bernstein." The head-cashier's response was a negative, "Sam, you're crazy if you become financially involved with Max Bernstein." Dad's reply was, "Mr. Madden, I appreciate your concern, but I am not here for a psychological analysis. Mr. Bernstein needs money and I am here to help him get it."

To make a long story a bit shorter, Max Bernstein went on to become a highly successful businessman and lifelong friend of my dad. He would attend services at Machzikeh HaDas on the High Holy Days and would pay $500 for Dad to say *Maftir Yonah*. Dad was influential in getting Maxi to fund needy Jews in many instances. If Maxi was not inclined to offer financial assistance, Dad would explain that the money that Maxi had did not really belong to him, that the Almighty has made him the executor of His estate. "Maxi," my dad would say, "Your job is to distribute G-d's money." Maxi would not refuse such an important job.

One instance in which Dad's influence was responsible for Maxi's financial help was in the case of Bess Levenberg. Bess, who was the daughter of a prominent *Rosh Yeshiva* and Torah scholar, was in need of treatment for a mental illness. She had been placed in a state institution, because she could not pay for private care. Dad prevailed on Maxi to fund private care for Bess. The medication that she received enabled her to eventually live on her own outside of an institution.

In compiling information about memories of Max Bernstein, Russi and I interviewed Maxi's son, Donny Bernstein in the office of his very successful business. Don recalled that as a youngster, he often accompanied his father to my dad's place of business, where Maxi would borrow money that he required for emergency business needs. Don recalled being confused as to who was lending money to whom. He was incredulous that Mr. Mintz was able to lend sizable amounts of money without so much as intimating that he was the lender. "I have been in business a while," Donny Bernstein said, "and I can honestly say I have never seen anything like it."

I would be remiss if I did not mention my dad's relationship with Joe Green. Joe was the son of Mrs. Green who was mentioned previously in this narrative, as the woman who frequented our house to sell her dry-goods to my mom. Joe was not well, I am not sure whether he would have been diagnosed with arrested development or with some form of mental illness. He would not have been capable of being hired for a regular job, but Dad hired him for errands and some light maintenance work. Dad paid him regular wages and saw to it that he was kept busy, but did not become overtired. One would think that Joe's family, the Jewish Family Service, and the Jewish community, would have been grateful that Joe was employed and not in any way burdensome to the community. Such was not the case however, it never ceased to amaze me how my dad's care for Joe Green was criticized from all sides. The Executive Director of Jewish Family Service called him to opine that the work wasn't appropriate. Shul members thought it might be dangerous because there were knives on the premises. The Bureau of Employment considered the work to be too strenuous. And even the Green family accused Dad of taking care of Joe for his own benefit. It should be emphasized that none of the aforementioned people had an alternate proposal or suggestion. When Dad passed away and the business was closed, Joe Green spent his remaining years in the Hillside Home which was a mental facility.

Previously mentioned was my dad's conception of a Jew, and perhaps equally meritorious was his concern for any person no matter his/her color, religion or station in life. Two instances are especially worthy of mentioning. Our store was frequented by men to whom my father referred as the "bottle gang." These people were basically drifters and existed on relief checks which they spent on alcohol. They asked Dad for money for food, but would spend it on alcohol. Instead of giving them money, which he knew would be detrimental to them, Dad made arrangements for them to eat at a luncheonette, the Mulberry Lunch, which was in the neighborhood. Dad would send anyone of those men who requested money for food to that luncheonette, which was not kosher, but which was owned by a Jew, Mr. Nussbaum. The owner was instructed to provide food for anyone who would ask for it. On his way home from work every evening, my dad would stop in the luncheonette to pay the bill.

I remember that one of the times when I was visiting in Scranton after I was married, I was walking with Dad as he was coming home from work, and we happened to see one of the bottle gang members. The man was called Mexican Joe, because he really was from Mexico and wore a huge sombrero. He was so drunk that he could hardly walk. Dad had tears in his eyes as he said to me, "This man is a human being, also made by G-d in His image. He just got his relief check this morning, but he already drank it up and now will starve for the rest of the month, money doesn't help him." My dad was wont to quote the *Gemarah*, "Every person is entitled to food. When one claims hunger we are required to feed him, no questions asked." This he put into practice every day of his life.

Besides being concerned with feeding these "bottle gang" members, Dad tried to help them improve their general well-being. He would talk to them about the importance of hearing about G-d and he tried to persuade them to go to church at least once a week. I remember one Sunday, when a regular "bottle gang" member came into the store. He had a really disgusted look on his face as he addressed my dad. "Mr. Sam," he said, "I just came from church, the priest was talking Latin and I don't know if he was buying me or selling me."

Dad's concern for the people in the neighborhood extended to helping the children who lived there. The parents of these children had the mistaken notion that the purpose of having a family was to claim additional government relief money to support them. The problem was that the money obtained for that purpose was in a good many cases spent on alcohol and things other than necessities for the family's existence. Children were ill-clothed, underfed and in many cases received medical attention that was at best inadequate, and more often nonexistent. There was even an instance in which eight children were sleeping in one bed, across the width of the bed. My dad would tell my siblings and me about the plight of these children and encourage us to share clothing, toiletries, even comic books with them. Equally as important as the material things that Dad brought from our house to these unfortunate children, was the time he spent talking to them. He would talk to them about school and ask to see their report cards. He would tell them how smart he knew they really were, and would offer them a dollar for each grade-improvement. In many cases, my dad's interest and encouragement resulted in these children's school-work improving from failing grades to honor-role status.

Dad's interest in these children was rewarded in an interesting way. One of the girls whom he had befriended was arrested for shoplifting. Dad was devastated when he heard about this, until he became aware of what had happened as a result. Because of her young age, the girl that had shoplifted was referred to Child Protective Services who investigated her situation. Upon discovering the condition of the home in which she was living, the social worker removed her from the home and put her in foster care. Further investigation resulted in the same being done with other children in the family, as well as in that neighborhood.

Two things that were essential to Dad's business, namely meat and raw materials for leather hides were rationed during the 1940s. These products were rationed for the military as World War II raged in Europe at that time. Prices that Dad could charge for meat were set by the OPA (the Office of Price Administration) as was the amount of meat that a family could purchase determined by the number of people. This regulation of the sale of meat made it impossible for the owner of a meat market to make a profit. Many kosher meat markets were simply forced out of business and none would accept new customers. In fairness to his customers, Dad did not close the store, but he did confine the business to one day a week for the duration of the war. As mentioned previously, the store was opened only on Thursdays.

The sale of hides had to be monitored by a government inspector who had to fill out a detailed form for each sale. On one occasion as the war progressed, Dad received a phone call from the state OPA inspector. He said from that time forward, Dad would be required to pay on each sale an amount to be specified by the OPA in order for the sale to be okayed by the government inspector. The reason for the new charge was that the government inspectors were accustomed to be paid money "under the table" in order to pass on a sale. Dad's reply was that he had earned his money with hard work, and suggested that the government inspectors do the same. He had never paid a bribe and he did not intend to do so.

Honesty had always been a vital part of Dad's existence, but in this case, it proved costly, after the next shipment, Dad received a letter from the OPA informing him that he had violated regulations in that shipment and that he was being fined several thousand dollars (I don't recall the exact figures). The letter did not address the fact that the shipment in question had been supervised by an OPA inspector who had signed a form verifying its accuracy. Dad personally went to the OPA office and informed them that he did not intend to pay the fine. "If I have broken the law then I belong in jail, because that is where one who breaks the law should be. Money has nothing to do with this case. I will present my case to the court, and the OPA should do the same. If the court finds me innocent then I go free, if the court finds me guilty, then I go to jail. This case is not about money."

Subsequent to Dad's appearance at the local OPA office, he received a series of letters from the OPA, each letter proposed a settlement reducing the fine. Dad's reply was always the same, "Uncle Sam does not do a hyphenated business. I am either guilty or not." The final letter from the OPA stated that the case had been dropped because the OPA office in Scranton was being closed. Needless to say my dad never paid any money to the OPA, nor did he receive any further demands to do so.

As mentioned previously, Dad's business consisted of curing hides before shipping them to tanneries in New England which manufactured shoes. The hides, which were picked up at the local slaughter houses, were highly perishable and had to be trimmed and salted immediately upon arrival at the hide house if they were not to spoil. This was especially true in hot weather. There were instances – especially before Shavuoth – when hide-pick-up was late afternoon and there was no time for salting before *yom tov*. The potential for monetary loss was great as the hides would remain unsalted for two days in the heat. It was however of no consequence to our Dad for whom the onset of any *yom tov* completely displaced any thought of business. The Yom Tov celebration went on with the usual excitement and dedication, it was only after *Havdallah* that Dad went to work in an attempt to salvage whatever merchandise he could, sometimes working through the night.

There was one instance that I particularly remember, in which the business connection did have an impact on our *Shabbos* celebration. Two representatives of a New England tannery who had come to Scranton to take up business with Dad, could not conclude their business on Friday, and had to stay in Scranton over *Shabbos*. Dad invited both men to our Friday night meal. Mr. Fine, who was Jewish, would go to shul on *Shabbos* with Dad, while Mr. Ditchett, who was not Jewish, stayed in the hotel. When he came home on *Shabbos* morning with Mr. Fine, Dad sent Moish and me to the hotel to invite Mr. Ditchett to lunch. Mr. Ditchett was deeply moved by our having made a special effort to include him in our Sabbath meal, since he was not Jewish. The subject that was discussed at the *Shabbos* table was Brotherhood Week which was being observed in the United States on that particular week. Mr. Ditchett noted that there was really no need for a week to focus on brotherhood for a family such as ours for whom brotherhood was observed all the time *(See Appendix K, Letter from Mr. Ditchett).*

CHAPTER 2
Childhood on Penn Avenue

As MENTIONED previously in this narrative, our first home was a third-floor apartment on the 300 block of Penn Avenue where we lived until I was about five years old. Actually there is only one memory that I have of this apartment. On *Shabbos* toward evening, we all sat together to sing the afternoon zmiros. Dad sat on his big wooden rocking chair and we children got on his lap two at a time, as we sang *Mizmor L'David, Attah Echod, Yismach Moshe, Ka Ribone,* and *Tzur Mishaloh.* All too soon the evening shadows grew increasingly darker and the time came for Dad to daven and make *Havdoloh.* We hated to see this beautiful time come to a close, but we comforted ourselves that G-d willing we would do it all again the following week.

Penn Avenue was a commercial district, composed mostly of wholesale businesses, owned by Jewish entrepreneurs. The store that I as a young child remember the most was Poller's Fish Market which was especially interesting because there were huge fish tanks with live fish swimming in them. Mrs. Poller who ran the business always wore rubbers since the floor was always wet. Mr. Poller was not well and sat on the sidelines most of the time. He frightened me because he had a box on his throat which caused him to speak in a way that was hard to understand. The Pollers were our neighbors as well since their apartment was on the second floor of our apartment building.

There were two shuls in the neighborhood, Penn Avenue Shul (the one to which my family belonged) and Linden Street Shul. Both were beautiful and well-attended by a relatively large Orthodox community.

In addition to the Pollers, the family in the neighborhood that I remember well were the Taylors. Mr. Taylor was a shoemaker whose place of business was on Mulberry Street around the corner from where we lived. It intrigued me that whenever we passed by the store, no matter the time of day, Mr. Taylor was always hard at work, pounding away at a shoe that he was repairing on a form right near the window. The only other members of the family that I saw were Mr. Taylor's wife and Pearl, the young daughter (about ten years of age). Mrs. Taylor was a sweet little lady with a lovely smile who seemed too old to have such a young child. Pearl seemed to have her mother's sweet temperament, always smiling and genuinely happy to be with her mother in the shoe repair shop. Pearl's hair was braided in a thick braid that was on her back and reached to her waist. Neither mother nor daughter had much in the way of worldly possessions but always seemed content to be in the store, enjoying each other's company. The Taylors were Jewish but had no relationship with the Jewish community. They were never in shul, not even on holidays, and did not even send their children, who in addition to their daughter, consisted of three sons, to Hebrew school.

Actually, the reason that I remember the Taylors so well was because of an incident that occurred after we had left Penn Avenue. Dad continued to daven in Penn Avenue shul during the week because his business was still in that neighborhood. Mr. Taylor passed away sometime later, and the Taylor sons came to shul every morning. Since they had probably never been to shul before and certainly had no Jewish education, they just sat and listened with no ability to participate in any way. My dad was not about to let this happen, and asked the Taylors if they would be willing to put on *tefilin* if he bought the *tefilin* and showed them how to put them on. When they enthusiastically answered in the affirmative, Dad did just that, and for the entire year, those three young men put on *tefilin* every day. Some in the shul thought that Dad had wasted his money since they posited that those *tefilin* would never be used once the year was over. Dad's reply, "I am not responsible for what the Taylors do in their own home, but I am responsible for helping Jews do the right thing when I am with them."

CHAPTER 3
Childhood on Webster Avenue

IN THE MIDDLE of my kindergarten year, when I was five years old, our family moved to Webster Avenue in the Hill section. Our new home consisted of ten rooms on three floors. It was a lovely residential neighborhood, in which all of the homes were either singles or doubles. Our only Jewish neighbor was the Horowitz family who lived around the corner on Mulberry Street. Since there was no day school in Scranton at that time, we all went to public school, James Madison, #33 on Quincy Avenue, four blocks from our home.

We were generally happy at Madison School; the academic level was good and the physical education department, which featured a beautiful big gym and a full line of sports equipment, was excellent. Our problem was the anti-Semitism which we had to deal with outside of school. On our way home for lunch each day, we encountered a group of rowdy neighborhood boys on their way to Chapel school. They would "accidentally" push or bump into all of us as they would pass by. But their main target was brother Moish, whom they actually, physically attacked. Moish would manage to get away each time, thankfully unhurt until the next time.

The solution to this problem came from Dad who offered Moish the following advice, "The next time one of those boys attacks you, hit him back and hit him hard. That is all he understands, if you hit him hard enough he will never bother you again and neither will anyone who is with him." I remember well the day Moish put this advice into practice. He knocked the boy down, grabbed his feet and dragged him with his head on the pavement. The boys never did bother us again.

The morning session of Madison School was 9AM until noon; the afternoon session was 1:30PM until 3:30PM. When we were old enough, we went directly to the Central Talmud Torah six blocks away at the YMHA on Wyoming Avenue. Hebrew classes for the younger children, which included brother Chaim, went from 4PM–5:30PM. While the latter group was in session, the rest of us had to wait our turn for our class which started at 5:30PM and concluded at 7PM. We would then walk three blocks to get the trolley car which took us home for an 8PM supper.

Even though the Hebrew classes made our school day so much longer, they were always inspirational and interesting. I remember looking forward to them each and every day. The teachers, Mr. Baruch Segal and Mr. Joseph Eisenberg faced the challenge each day of teaching children who were tired after a long day in school, and would certainly have preferred some recreation to spending more time in class. Besides a genuine love for the children, Mr. Segal and Mr. Eisenberg were deeply committed to doing as much as they could to mold a generation of Jewish adults who were observant, knowledgeable, and a credit to the Jewish people. We children were impressed daily with the importance of learning and how terrible it would be to be an ignorant Jew. They told stories and even jokes to illustrate this point. Mr. Segal was proud of the fact that he had been born in Israel, and both he and Mr. Eisenberg inculcated in us a love for *Eretz Yisrael* in all that they taught.

A major incentive to learning was the weekly appearance of Rabbi Guterman, the chief Orthodox rabbi in Scranton who came every Thursday to examine the classes. Everyone felt the need to apply him/herself all week so as to perform well on Thursday. When we completed the book of *Beraishis*, Rabbi Guterman offered a $5.00 cash award for any student who memorized the *Sedras Vayegash* and *Vayechi*. I was ten years old at the time and very excited at the prospect of earning $5.00. At the end of what seemed like a very long time and a lot of hard work, the time for the memory test was at hand. As luck would have it, I had the flu with a fever of 102 degrees. I begged and pleaded to be allowed to go just for the test. I would bundle up and come back right after the test was over. Mom was sympathetic but firm, "You have to think of others," she said, "You are sick and will spread your germs to the other children." When Rabbi Guterman was told of my plight, he sent a message assuring me that he would give me a special test as soon as I felt better.

That long awaited day arrived at last. I recited the *Birchas Yaakov* by memory for Rabbi Guterman and was awarded a crisp new five-dollar bill. Needless to say, it was with much pleasure and a great deal of excitement that I showed my prize to my parents and siblings. I was however a bit taken aback when Dad asked what I intended to do with the money. That had never been a consideration, in fact it never even occurred to me, I had no clue and said as much. Dad suggested a gift for the Jewish Home. He rightly pointed out that Mother's Day which was approaching would be a time when some of the Home's residents would be remembered by their families while others would not. He suggested that I order a box of apples and oranges from Genovese Fruit Market, which sold superior quality fruit. "You can get a big box of fruit for that amount of money," he said. "Every time one of the old people in the home takes a bite of the fruit you send and gets *hana'ah* from it, you get *Olam Habba*. Just imagine how much *Olam Habba* you can get for $5.00."

I ordered the fruit and went with the driver in my dad's truck to pick it up and deliver it to the Jewish Home. Some days later, I received a letter from Roslyn Burnat Kerber, the Executive Director at the Home (*See Appendix L*), praising my gift as the most appreciated thing the residents had received for Mother's Day. "We realize that it must have been a sacrifice for you to spend that amount of money ($5.00 was a lot of money in 1945), and we applaud your decision to do so." I gave the letter to my dad since as I told him it really should have been addressed to him in the first place. I was the messenger but the idea had been his. At that point, my dad handed me a crisp new $5.00 bill. "I didn't want you to give away that money for which you worked so hard, I just wanted you to know that money is only important because of the good that you can do with it. It is a medium of exchange and in and of itself is meaningless." I guess I had learned that lesson well, since that $5.00 which just a short time before had been so important to me, was now something that I did not even want.

Growing up in Scranton, when we were young children, really meant that out social contacts were basically limited to family. We looked forward to *Shabbos* as something very sacred and special. It was always important to help in the house or to run errands. But to do so *l'kavod Shabbos*, was a distinct privilege and something that no child would have ever been less than enthusiastic about doing. My brother Chaim set the *erev Shabbos* schedule with the proposal that the girls will do the housework and the boys will do the errands. Zip assisted Mom in the kitchen, I cleaned the house and the boys did do the errands. Friday night the whole family *davened* together and who can ever forget the *L'cha Dodi* which we sang with all our might. The *Shabbos* meals were all festive occasions and went on for hours. This was the time when we children would talk about all the happenings of the week. If it was important to us, then it was important to our parents as well. The *zmiros* were legendary and could be heard throughout the neighborhood in the warm weather when the windows were open. *Shabbos* afternoons we all sat around the table saying *Tehilim* one *pasuk* each until the *yom* was finished. By then it was usually time for *seudah shlishis* and so the *Shabbos* went. I don't think that it occurred to any of us that maybe we should do something else on *Shabbos* afternoon, and if it did, no one ever said so.

There is one particular *Shabbos* that stands out in my memory, because it is illustrative of the esteem in which our Dad held *Shabbos*.

Our cousins the German family, were making an *aufruf* in honor of the forthcoming marriage of Leonard German. Leonard was the son of Mary German, the daughter of Mordechai Yoseph Mintz (better known in the family as the *Fetter Mutta*). Dad was the only one who would be attending the *aufruf* because it was being held in the Flats which was too far for us children to walk. In order to be on time for shul, Dad left the house at 7:30 AM and was not expected home before 1 or 2 in the afternoon. Imagine our shock and surprise when he returned home at 11 o'clock. In a nonchalant manner Dad explained that since Leonard's father was not a well person (he had been ill for some years) it was decided to move things along very quickly. In answer to our questions, he told us about family members who were in attendance and described the *kiddush* with a detailed account of what was served and how it was set up. Not until after *Havdala* did we learn what actually had happened. There had been no *aufruf* at all because Leonard's Dad had passed away at 6 o'clock in the morning. Unwilling to disturb our *Shabbos* with sad news. Dad just invented the *aufruf*. Most amazing however was the way he pulled it off. No trace in either his manner or his speech showed that he had come from sadness, not from a *simcha*.

Another very memorable occasion in our house was the *erev Yom Kippur* meal that went on for hours. Our Bubbi would bake a special *challah* which she decorated with birds and ladders. She would explain to us children that ladders would reach to Heaven and the birds would carry our prayer to G-d. Simultaneously with the meal, the radio was playing in an adjoining room broadcasting the World Series. We children were very much concerned with the World Series and went back and forth from the dinner table to the radio in order to keep abreast of the game. At no point did our Dad or Zaida object or direct us to turn the radio off and remain seated at the table. At the appropriate time, our dad told us it was time to *bentsch* and we knew that as was our custom, we would *bentsch* aloud together. As we proceeded with the *bentsching* our focus was increasingly on Dad who looked different than how we had ever seen him. He did not actually cry, but his eyes were red and his demeanor conveyed the seriousness of the moment, more than anything he could have said.

I must admit that we did get back to the game after *bentsching*. But the point had been made. None of us even remember who had played in that ballgame. But we had learned a lifelong lesson about *erev Yom Kippur*.

There is another lesson from this period that I particularly remember and would like to share. As mentioned previously my dad did the bookkeeping for the business himself. He did have an accountant, but that was only because he was less likely to be audited by the IRS if the accountant's name were signed on his tax return. He used to say that he did the math himself because he didn't want anyone to tell him how much money he had. When he had completed the figuring, Dad would dictate the problems to me over the phone and we would compare answers. On the rare occasions that I found that he had made an error, his effusive praise of me made me feel like a million dollars. When we did the figuring for federal taxes, we would work together in Dad's office. On one such occasion on a Thursday night, when we had just finished our work, Mom called to say that she needed me to mail a package to my brothers in the yeshiva. As was her custom, Mom would send a package of baked goods to Moish and Chaim for every *Shabbos*. In those days, a package could be sent from the rear of the post office until 8PM every evening. Since it was already after 7PM and since Dad had some errands to do, I rushed home by myself.

I was half a block from the house, when I noticed an elderly woman, who seemed to be in a hysterical state, holding onto a building. She pleaded with me to help her get home. On impulse, I took her arm for what I thought would be a short distance to her home.

As we walked, I realized the foolishness of what I was doing. I was walking with a stranger in the dark for three blocks, one of which turned out to be a dark alley. When, with a sigh of relief, I finally got her home, I ran home as fast as I could. I found my parents in a virtual state of panic. They could think of no logical explanation for the fact that I had been rushing to get home a distance of six blocks and had not arrived an hour later. The fact that I was okay was all that mattered, but as was their custom, they took advantage of the occasion to teach an important lesson: Helping a fellow human being is always important, but equally important is giving that help in a way that is equally beneficial to the giver as well as to the receiver. In my case, the best way to help would have been to give the woman a chair on our porch, while I called 911 and arranged someone to take her home. Helping does not necessarily mean "doing it yourself." A simple lesson perhaps, but one that has been a benefit to me many times since.

Chapter 4
Madison Avenue

In 1952, Dad bought the house on Madison Avenue where we live now. It was the first house he had ever owned, all of the previous residences having been rented. The cost of the house was $10,000, which Dad paid in cash. Location was the main reason for choosing this particular house. Since we did not own a car, it was important to be in walking distance of the *shul*, bus and train stations, two supermarkets and the downtown shopping area. Also within walking distance was Central High School which both Zip and I attended at the time.

An added bonus concerning the Madison Avenue location was the fact that the house was one house away from Rabbi Guterman's house. My dad happily told us that living near to Rabbi Guterman took him back to his early days in Scranton when the Mintz family and the Gutermans were neighbors and the two families became good friends. Dad's friendship with Simeon and Abe Guterman remained steadfast all of their lives, even though they probably only saw one another on the rare occasion when the Gutermans visited Scranton. The esteem in which they held Dad is evidenced in the letters which they sent on Dad's passing (*See Appendix M*).

At the time that we moved to Madison Avenue, my brothers were both at Ner Israel in Baltimore, and Zip was in college in New York where she boarded with cousins Debbie and Felix Taubenblatt. I decided on Wilkes College so that I could live at home. Wilkes was a small liberal arts school, which had until a short time before been Bucknell Junior College. I had delayed applying, because I was undecided as to whether I wanted to take the bus to Wilkes Barre every day or if I preferred Marywood in Scranton. Even though I was late in applying, I received a call from the registrar's office to schedule an appointment. Mr. Whitby, the registrar, offered to convene a meeting of the scholarship committee to get me a full four-year scholarship to Wilkes. I was delighted at the prospect of saving my family so much money and was impatient to give them the good news. Dad was proud that my honor roll status in Central (I graduated seventh in my class of 357) had made me eligible for this scholarship, but he did not want me to accept it. "I saved money for your college education," he said, "You will go without a scholarship. But schools have limited funds. If you take the money there may then not be enough left for some needy student who will be denied a college education." That was vintage Dad. Work hard for years to send your own child to college, but don't risk denying that opportunity to some else.

Graduate school for me was at Fordham University, School of Social Work in New York City. I lived at home and took the train to New York at 5AM on Wednesdays for Wednesday and Thursday classes. My field work was at the Family Service of Lackawanna County in Scranton during the remaining days of the week. It was a difficult schedule, but the program was challenging, and the work was both interesting and rewarding. The only problem was my case-work supervisor Eleanor. She was a conservative Jewess, and from the beginning made religion an issue. She reasoned that since we were the only Jewish Social workers in the agency, we should present a united front in regard to religious observance. My suggestion that we focus on social work practice and make no reference to religious philosophy and/or observance fell on deaf ears. Eleanor's continued focus on religion had a negative impact on her critique of my work. The result was that her reports to the school did not give me as high a score as I deserved. My only recourse was to apprise my advisor at Fordham of the problem with Eleanor and to request a different case-work supervisor. I reasoned that since my work at the agency involved considerable effort and a sizable amount of money, I had every right to request a supervisor who would be fair in her assessment of my work. Here again, my dad's reliance on principle came into play: "You have every right to report what Eleanor's doing," he said, "But you should not do so. It is forbidden for a Jew to report a fellow Jew to a non-Jew, that is the law, no matter how right you are." The work was mine, but the money spent on my education was my dad's money, for which he had worked very hard. Once again, as he demonstrated all of his life, he lived by principle. Money was something that was necessary to sustain life, but would never supersede the right thing to do.

PART III–INTERVIEWS

VIDEO TRANSCRIPTIONS

RUTH LEITER: Welcome to the Mintz Family Reunion 2006. I want to tell you briefly why I put together this documentary.

The past few years that we've come together for the reunions, we've spoken about Bubbi and Zaidy, and what I learned has made a great impact on my life. But I thought that it would be interesting to interview people who are not members of the family. My favorite saying of Zaidy's is, "Your life is your plaque", meaning that is doesn't matter what diplomas are on your wall, or what certificates you have been awarded. How you live and who you are, is how people remember you. With this thought in mind, I interviewed some people who interacted with Bubbi and Zaidy over the years and had come to know them well.

I met Phil Harris in the bakery last summer, and I said to him, "Mr. Harris, tell me something about my grandfather." Seemingly very much overwhelmed with the question, he said, "There's too much to say, not enough time now, but I can assure you that you will never know half the wonderful things that your grandfather did." Likewise when I asked Betty Stahler if she could say anything about Bubbi, she said "That is too big of a question; so let me just say, she was a beautiful person, and a true fine lady."

One of the people that I interviewed was Moshe Fink.

MR. MOSHE FINK:

RL: I know that you are so much younger than my grandfather was, but do you know if there was a feeling or a thought that would go through people's minds when they would speak of Sam Mintz? Did you ever hear anything?

MF: Yeah there were a couple of things. He was a legend in his own time for a couple of reasons. One of them is that he ran a one-man gemach, that if somebody was short of money, one could approach him in times when cash was very tight. He generally had money that was available for the asking. There was no surety or safety deposit, it was simply that you said you needed it, you would pay it and you got it. I'm certain that not all of it was repaid but he never kept a record, he never asked anyone for the money so that if it was out there and it was not paid he didn't come looking for someone to repay it.

He was larger than life. When I was growing up there were stories that he was a pillar in the Scranton community, but he was a pillar that was built into the structure that you never saw. He was not flamboyant – saying flamboyant and Sam Mintz in the same sentence is a contradiction in terms – but he was very influential in the community because of his contact with everybody. Everybody in the Jewish and non-Jewish community knew him. He was a very strong influence in the Orthodox community because of the low profile personality that he was. People would go to him for questions – about loans of course, like I mentioned, but also for advice because he was a very knowledgeable person. His common sense was a very fundamental part of his nature.

RL: What do you know about my grandmother?

MF: As you are probably aware, my mother, may she rest in peace, and your grandmother, may she rest in peace, were close acquaintances. Over the years I got the distinct feeling from my mom that Laura Mintz stood as a role model, or perhaps a paragon of living Yiddishkeit in a contemporary world. She was not pushy; she was not tremendously outgoing in her personality; but she had a rock solid faith, and steadfastness of purpose that made a very strong impression on my mother's conduct. My mom had come from a quite modern home, and of the people in Scranton who had a strong influence, I would say that Laura Mintz was one of the most influential. My mom kind of modeled her existence on Mrs. Mintz's conduct and it was something that was brought home very strongly to me in my growing up years.

Dr. David Horowitz:

RL: Another interview was conducted with Dr. Horowitz.

I never knew my grandfather, yet it's amazing because I feel that in my own life, when things happen, I think "What would Zaidy say about that?" And even though he passed away 23 years before I was born, I really feel that I knew him. However, I know that you are one of the people who actually did know him, so if you were thinking back, what would be the first thing that would come to your mind about him? A word or a phrase, or something that you associate with my grandfather.

Dr. H: You have to remember that my memory of your grandfather takes place when I was a little kid, when I was running around to the movies with Mosey and Herbie. So it was always in association with them that I remember him. First of all, I spent a tremendous amount of time in your grandmother's house on Webster Avenue. As kids would at that time, we would turn the house upside down with pillows… and after we had quieted down a bit we would take a piece of white chalk and smack in the middle of a red carpet, make something like this (demonstrates a circle). Then Herbie would get on one side and I would get on the other side and we would play marbles, and your grandmother never said a word. Never! That was just fine. "You want to play marbles? Go ahead, very nice. Would you like a lemonade while you're playing marbles? Would you like something to drink?"

I remember mostly your grandfather as a wonderfully warm, accepting person. Everybody had a certain *chashivus* in his eyes, and he greeted everybody very much the same way. People were very dear to him, he liked people although he was not a big talker and not a big socializer. He didn't sit in shul after davening and *shmooze* and gab. He came to shul, and after *davening*, he picked himself up and he walked home. And that's all. But when I say "accepting", I know of course because I was told, that there were dozens of people in town for whom he lent significant amounts of money for nothing more than their word. "You'll pay me back next month." How many times has Jerry Ganz told me when he first came to town and he didn't have more than two nickels to rub together how many times your grandfather had given him money. And for one project he borrowed and he returned the money a few days before the due date because he was paid, and just wanted to return the money. Your grandfather looked at him and said "Are you sure you don't want a few more days? It was nothing to him. This one, that one, the other one... So many people. Didn't ask about your Brad Street rating, didn't inquire about your credit worthiness, or whether your grandfather was frum or not frum- if you needed something, this was an address to go to.

In very much the same way there used to be this Mulberry Lunch that was on Mulberry Street on the outside of the street near the old State Hospital. I also remember that sometimes that Mosey, Herbie and I would go down to the hide cellar. There was not a worse smell in the world than that hide cellar. But whenever we came down he would stop what he was doing and say "Yes, gentlemen?" We would say "We would like to see Roy Rogers this afternoon. Can we have 25 cents to see Roy Rogers?" and he would say, "Would Roy Rogers pay 25 cents to come see you?" Of course that brought a smile to everybody and we'd say "No…" "So why are you paying 25 cents to go see Roy Rogers?" "Well, he has a nice horse…" "Oh… he has a nice horse." He had the ability to make you feel worthy. It wasn't, "Kid you're pestering me, can't you see I'm working?" That was never the kind of talk that came from him. Whoever was there was a valuable G-d creation and he treated them as such. Whether you were big or small, *frum* or not *frum*, long *tzitzis* or no *tzizis*, you know you had a feeling that this was a man who…

So I was telling you the story of this luncheon. I remember many times being in the cellar and somebody would come in there, some real down-and-outer –*shikkur*, not *shikkur*, Jew, not Jew… and he came and started to tell your grandfather his trouble. This and that… The first thing he would do is look them in the eye and ask "Are you hungry? When was the last time you ate?" And half of them would say yesterday or last week. So he'd say "Go over to that luncheonette and tell them that Sam sent you." And they would go and Sam would settle out his bill once a week, or once a month, depending on how much business they would do.

RL: It's funny because my brother Yechiel was telling us during the last reunion that he learned during the first reunion to give people time. Because he has a lot of people who come into his office, and he doesn't have time for everybody. And then once in a while someone would come in with whom he has no reason to spend any time with and he would think, "Our Zaidy would spend time with this person." He would spend time with him regardless of his stature, and Yechiel would be surprised sometimes about what he would get out of it.

Dr. H: He would always stop his work, whatever he was doing, and come and talk to you, greet you. You have to understand that this was heavy, hard work, and that when he would stop working, the other employees would stop working too. But there was a person who needed him, so it was worth it to him to stop the work. About 25-30 years ago I learned the *hakdama* to *Sefer Beraishis* from the *Netziv's Chumash*, and as soon as I learned it, I got goosebumps. To all of your uncles who are *talmidei chachamim*, let them look up the *Netziv* themselves. You can also – maybe this Friday you will as well. He says that *Beraishis* is called *Sefer Hayashar*, because it is a recounting of the lives of the *yesharim*. What is a *yashar*? A *yashar* is someone who is straight, not devious, for whom *tzedaka* and kindness is something that is for everyone. And regardless of who you are – when Avraham had a tent that was open from three sides, he didn't have a *tzizis* inspection before you came into his tent. That's how it was and that's who he was. And so *Avraham* is called a *yashar*. Learn it.

The first time I read it I thought "I know who this is. This is Mr. Mintz."

RL: I also heard that your mother used to go toward the end of every *Yom Tov* to the Mintz house because she used to say that she wanted to spend the last few hours of *Yom Tov* at their house. Do you know why that is?

DR. H: I remember that my mother and your grandmother would spend the last few hours of *yom tov* together. Your grandmother used to come to our house at the *neilas hayom tov* – when the *yom tov* left. She would sit in the room and my mother would make her a tea, and they would sit and schmooze as the shadows were gathering and it was getting darker. The room was dark, and for the life of me I never understood this, I just had a feeling that there was something very close going on, but as I kid I never understood what was going on. The whole ambiance – the cup of tea, the gathering shadows, sitting about this distance they would sit and talk to each other, very quietly, very reverently. Now these two people were about as far from one another as I am from the moon. Your grandmother was an American-born product, and she went to college. My mother came from the hinterlands of Hungary where she was sopped full with *Chassidishe* lore and stories, but it didn't make any difference. There was a *kesher* of the heart. They were dedicated to their families and that's what their life was. They were also the only two ladies in Scranton who wore a *shaitel* at the time. And it was a very nice thing. My mother would say, "Mrs. Mintz is here," and they would close the door and sit by themselves, and it was very nice. Then on the other *yom tov* she would go to Webster Avenue. I don't know if they would do the same thing there but I would imagine that they sat in the gathering shadows of the *yetzias hachag*. Yes that's it – "*But leitenet yom tov mit Mrs. Mintz.*"

RL: We always talk about how now materialistic things are very important to children and people. One thing I heard about my grandfather is that money was "A medium of exchange" – important because of the good that you can do with it. It's not valuable in and of itself.

Dr. H: At that time he was looked upon as a person who had. Now, I don't know what that means – had what? Had 1 thousand, had 100 thousand – I don't know what "had" means. But regardless of what he did have, certainly you never knew that from his standard of living. The way his children dressed was not any different than the way my father's children dressed, and my father was a very poor man. They looked the same. The Mintz kids walked out, and so did Chazzan Horowitz's kids – they looked the same. The fact that he had made no difference because it wasn't important to him to have a fancy house or... to the best of my knowledge he never owned a car. Now surely

I would think that he would have been able to afford a car if he so wished, but he probably felt that this was unnecessary. You know, if he had a choice of having a car or lending money to Jerry Ganz or the likes of that, he'd rather lend the money.

RL: But he did like nice things. They only had one bike, but it was a nice one.

DH: It was a Schwinn. That Schwinn bike at various times used to carry about six people. Either I or Moishy sat in the seat, somebody else stood on the hoop, somebody stood on the handlebar, somebody stood on the pedals. That bike went all over the place – that blue Schwinn.

One thing I remember is that on *Shabbos* afternoon he would sit in the den and drink tea. Your grandmother used to make him tea but he drank it in a ball jar. He used to drink tea in a quart ball jar. And he had a little *sefer* in his hand – I don't know if it was a *Tehillim* or a *Chumash*, whatever it was. And he would sit there with the *sefer* and drink his tea on *Shabbos* afternoon in his chair after his nap which is where he used to sit with his big ball jar. And I would wonder why does he have to drink it in a ball jar? But that's the way he used to drink tea – in a ball jar. To the best of my knowledge he was not a learner but I don't think that I have ever heard *zemiros* sung at a table with as much love and feeling as I do remember at his table. He – "*aufen hoichen kol*" as loud as he could and he had a nice voice – he had a strong voice and everybody would sing and his love of zemiros was very infectious because all of the kids were involved in the singing. Now we lived on the 1200 block of Mulberry. They lived on the 300 block of Webster –around the corner. On a nice day we could hear the *zemiros* from Sam Mintz's house all the way to our house. We could hear them singing *zemiros* on Friday night.

It was just like a real unvarnished, *emesdike simcha* of being *yid*. I wish I could find some more people like that who could demonstrate to me the happiness that they had had just to sit at the table with their children and sing *zemiros* as loud as they could. Occasionally I would be there for *Shabbos* and I would witness that that complete abandon, that complete absorption in the happiness of the moment. And that always came, I always remembered that. He was a person who was happy to be Avraham and Yitzchak's grandson. He was very happy about that. He sang about it, and conducted himself that way.

RL: My mother said that people would come to the butcher shop collecting money and he would say "Okay, but let me hear a *vort*. I know you sit and learn, I want to hear something." He would have such *nachas* from people who dedicate their lives to Torah and could educate him. And he loved it so much.

DH: He was a certain unvarnished, non-fake person. There was nothing fake about him, nothing ever put-on… He was just a very happy camper. He worked hard; he worked extremely hard – long hours in a very hard business.

Mr. Sam Harris:
RH: Mr. Harris, tell me what you know about my grandfather.

PH: Anybody in the Orthodox community above the age of 18 had to know about your grandfather R' Zalman. I mean he was a *shem tov* – an outstanding man. The respect that that man had in the community was unbelievable. I'm not trying to exaggerate. I was a young man, but R' Zalman was looked up to as a paradigm of what a person should really be. And one incident that I do remember my father recounting about your grandfather was that he was a great *baal tzedaka*. And I remember that one time a *meshulach* came to your grandfather about three days before Rosh Hashana and your grandfather was a gentle man but he was upset, and he said to this man from *Yerushalayim* – "What are you doing here?" He said "What do you mean?" So he said "It's three days before *Yom Tov*, you should be in Israel preparing for *Yom Tov*", in a spiritual sense. And that's just to give you a sense of how he felt about *Yom Tov* coming up and how a person should prepare himself spiritually for the holiday. And here's this *meshulach* who needed money, but in your grandfather's eyes it was more important for this *meshulach* to be in *Yerushalayim* preparing. I don't know another man, frankly, who had the respect and reputation that your grandfather had. My father was a well-respected man *alav hashalom*, but he wasn't looked at on the same level as your grandfather was – he was one of a kind. And I just wish that we would have had many more people like your grandfather. For me it was an honor and a privilege to have known him. I remember when he passed away in 1954 I believe, I would normally daven at Machazikei Hadas but that particular *Shabbos* I was sick. And I don't know if my wife went to *shul* but when they came back they told us, the entire town found out about it and I was so upset that of all the days to get sick, I wasn't there to see him. But I'm sure I was at the funeral. I can't repeat myself enough to say that it was an honor for me to have known him and a privilege for me to have lived in the same community as he did.

RL: The importance of the interview that I did with Naomi Feder speaks for itself.

Mrs. Naomi Feder:

My name is Naomi Feder. I am Sam and Laura's niece. My father, Max Jacob was the second in the family, Uncle Sam was the oldest. Even though we were a significant distance from one another – Scranton to Flatbush – for some reason, I was the closest with Uncle Sam and Aunt Laura and therefore would go there on my own when I was older and able to travel and so established an independent relationship with them. I knew them better than I knew the other aunts and uncles. I admired them tremendously, as well as their kids. We were closer to you than the other kids who lived much closer to us.

I remember Uncle Sam more clearly than your mother, Aunt Laura. I think I had more to do with him for some reason. I was always impressed with the fact that he was able to talk to people and talk straight. That he was able to relate to people honestly, and would listen to you. He was very committed to the things he was committed to. He was straight and honest, and I remember the community really admiring and loving him for who he was. But there must have been something more personal between himself and me. It must have been the fact that I felt so understood, connected and liked. There was a personal quality of connectedness that he was able to have with me, and if he could have it with me then he would have had it with others too. It wasn't warm fuzziness- he did not speak in lengthy words. He was short, to the point and very real. And there was a warmth in the way he was able to connect to people. And I think that is what brought me back there. And I was always very welcomed in that house. Your mom too. Very welcoming and the one big anecdote that I have about that is that I was in Camp Moshava and we were kids, maybe 16, 17, and it was between sessions so we were off one day and there was a truck that was going from camp to Scranton. We hitched onto the bus, a whole bunch of us, spending the day in Scranton having a ball and into the nighttime. Then we realized that it was 11 or 12 and we said 'How are we going to get back to camp?' We were stranded in Scranton, we were kids so we didn't have any money, and I had this great idea – "I know! I have an aunt and uncle in Scranton." We must have been 10-12 people. We went to Uncle Sam and Aunt Laura and all of my friends hid behind trees, in the shrubbery, and I was sent to knock on the door. Uncle Sam answered and I said "I am stranded in Scranton. What am I going to do?" And Uncle Sam said "Absolutely- Naomi come in." I said, "Well I happen to have a few friends who happen to be with me". And then like munchkins they all come out of the bushes – 10 or 12, one after the other. My Aunt Laura nearly had a fit. But Uncle Sam said come on in. This was Uncle Sam – he would never in a million years not let us in. Would never say a word that would make me feel bad or imposing. That's a certain special kind of quality. He let us all come in, and we slept on the floor. It was wall to wall people on the floor. Early in the morning he went out and bought bread to make sandwiches.

There was another story that I particularly remember. I was probably about 18-19 or something like that, and my friend Kaddish and I met at the George Washington Bridge – I don't know how my parents let us do this – and we started to hitch over the bridge to Scranton. When I got to your father's house, he was astonished. I mean rightly so – this was not something that should've have been done. I remember that we were going to hitch back. Your father took me into his study and closed the door, almost like an Andy Hardy sort of thing. I knew when the door closed, in no way was I going to be permitted to hitch back - he was adamant.

RL: How did my Zaidy feel about his responsibility as the oldest sibling?

There were members of the family who needed additional help, and Uncle Sam undertook to help them. My father did as well – the two of them were the helpers. That was who he was. He was responsible for me and my munchkin friends; he was responsible for me when I hitched and he was not going to let me hitch back. It was a kind of carrying authority and responsibility. He was in charge and was going to carry this responsibility no matter what.

Your parents made a wonderful couple. Uncle Sam was to all outside appearances the dominant one. He was sure of himself – assertive when he said something. And he came forth and took control of situations as this indicated. But I remember your mother as a quiet strength. Kind of behind the throne. Firm, gentle, but a strength behind it. And a force that your father had to reckon with. It was not like he did things unilaterally without her input and she was always kind of an even keel, a steadying force there while your father was more assertive and out there. She was more quiet, but very much maintained the equilibrium in the family.

PART IV

SPEECH BY RABBI MAX MINTZ
On the Occasion of Dov's Bar-Mitzvah

I asked Uncle Max to speak at Dov's Bar-Mitzvah, to tell Dov about the grandfather for whom he was named. Unfortunately, Uncle Max broke his wrist and was unable to attend the Bar-Mitzvah. He did record his message, and that message is transcribed here.

To MY DEAR AND DARLING NEPHEW, Zalman Dov ben Noson Tzvi Leiter, *chaviv v'yakar*. The first time in my life experiences I'm addressing a bar mitzvah long distance via recording. On the supernatural scene of Torah giving on Mount Sinai the passage reads. "*V'chol haam roim es hakolos*"– And all of the people saw the voices and the words of the commandments that were uttered from Heaven downward. Though rare, there are moments in life when we see in vision, words and things that are naturally only heard by ear. As I address these words to you Zalman Dov, I see you through loving eyes I visualize the radiant faces of your dear parents, loving grandparents, and dear family emanating joy and *simcha*, Yes, in a spiritual form beyond the description of words I feel the presence of your sainted grandfather for whom you are named, Zalman Dov. So distance is erased and in the nearness of sentiment and emotion I say these words. You are the son combining the double heritage of two notable families. Torah found a repository through their many generations. "*Torah machzeres al achsanya shela*" – the Torah, word of G-d and spiritual inspiration always return generation after generation after it was received with welcome, studied with dedication and followed as a guiding light through the way of Jewish life. You are blessed Zalman Dov, and you are most fortunate. You have wonderful parents to follow and to emulate in their pattern of life. You are blessed with a father fully ordained as a rabbi and rich in the storage of Torah learning, which is his due reward for the many dedicated years that he spent in its study. May I add in close association with this that your dear and beloved mother was the only student in a class that pursued higher Jewish education, far beyond that of Talmud Torah standards under the tutelage and instruction of the sainted Rabbi Guterman who said of her that he had yet to see her likes in mind, heart, and soul. Your dear parents, both of them, have you shown you the ways that are good. You have teachers that have and are inspiring you on a high level of Torah. And to you belongs the greatest measure of credit for responding voluntarily and linking yourself in a long chain of Torah tradition that belongs to both families of your inheritance. And finally Zalman Dov, my thoughts, my sentiments and my message would be incomplete without a brief evaluation and memorial tribute to your sainted maternal grandfather for whom you are named. And my older brother, of blessed memory. To sum up his life and his enviable good traits of nature. I would refer to Rabbi Yochanan son of Zachai who had five disciples. He said to them go forth, praise and each one of you bring back an attribute that would lead to a good life. Rabbi Eliezer said "*ayin tova*" – a good eye. An eye that sees the good in every person. The eye that does not rouse envy or jealousy in the blessings of other people. Rabbi Yehoshua said "*chaver tov*" – be a good friend. Be a friend who brings joy and satisfaction. Being a good friend makes friends who share with you the warm blessings of joy and satisfaction. Rabbi Yosi said "*shachen tov*" – a good neighbor. Being a good neighbor you can serve them day and night. Both when the sun of fortune shines on them and even at night when misfortune strikes, *chas veshalom*. Rabbi Shimon said "One who foresees the reward of good deeds and the punishment of bad deeds". Rabbi Eliezer said "In all thy thoughts and deeds know this: there is an eye that sees, an ear that hears and all your deeds are written down in a book written by your own hand". All of this together, that was Zalman Mintz. He shunned *kavod*, honor. He ran from it all his life and he certainly does not ask for it or need it now. It is written on the hearts and minds of hundreds who are here and who were here and are no longer here. You have his name, Zalman Dov, now go his ways and emulate his deeds. And in the long years to come, and in the world in which you live and activate and function, men will say of you, you were a blessed man in this world and your reward will be rich in the world to come. *Mazel tov* and G-d bless you.

PART V – APPENDICES

APPENDIX A: Declaration of Intention

2843

Form 2203

U. S. DEPARTMENT OF LABOR
NATURALIZATION SERVICE

TRIPLICAT
[To be given to the]
the Declarat

No. 28403

UNITED STATES OF AMERICA

DECLARATION OF INTENTION

☞ Invalid for all purposes seven years after the date hereof

State of Pennsylvania, } ss.: In the Court of Quarter Sessions of Philadel
County of Philadelphia, } County, Pennsylvania.

I, _Laura Kramer_ _____, aged _19_ y
occupation ____ _Student_ _____, do declare on oath that my pers
description is: Color white, complexion ___ _fair_ ___, height _5_ feet _2_ inc
weight _112_ pounds, color of hair _brown_, color of eyes _Gray_
other visible distinctive marks ___ _none_ ___
I was born in ___ _Kuen Russia_ ___
on the _25_ day of _Dec_ _____, anno Domini 1_899_; I now re
at _1221 N. 91 St._ _____, Philadelphia,
                        (Give number and street)
I emigrated to the United States of America from _Riga Russia_ ___
on the vessel _Caernic_ _____; my
            (If the alien arrived otherwise than by vessel, the character of conveyance or name of transportation company should be given)
foreign residence was _Riga Russia_ _____; I am _not_ married; the na
of my wife is _____; she was born at _____
and now resides at _____
It is my bona fide intention to renounce forever all allegiance and fidelity to any fore
prince, potentate, state, or sovereignty, and particularly to _____
_____, of whom I am now a subje
I arrived at the port of _____ _Boston_ _____, in
State of _____ _Mass._ _____, on or about the _24_
of _____ _Sept._ _____, anno Domini 1_906_; I am not an anarchist; I am no
polygamist nor a believer in the practice of polygamy; and it is my intention in good fa
to become a citizen of the United States of America and to permanently reside there
SO HELP ME GOD.

Laura Kramer
(Original signature of declarant)

Subscribed and sworn to before me in the office of the Clerk of said Co
[SEAL]   at Philadelphia, Pa., this _7_ day of _Nov._
            anno Domini 191 9

Thomas W. Cunningham

Clerk of the Court of Quarter Sess

By _John G. Kirchhess_, Assistant Cle

106

Appendix B: Petition for Naturalization

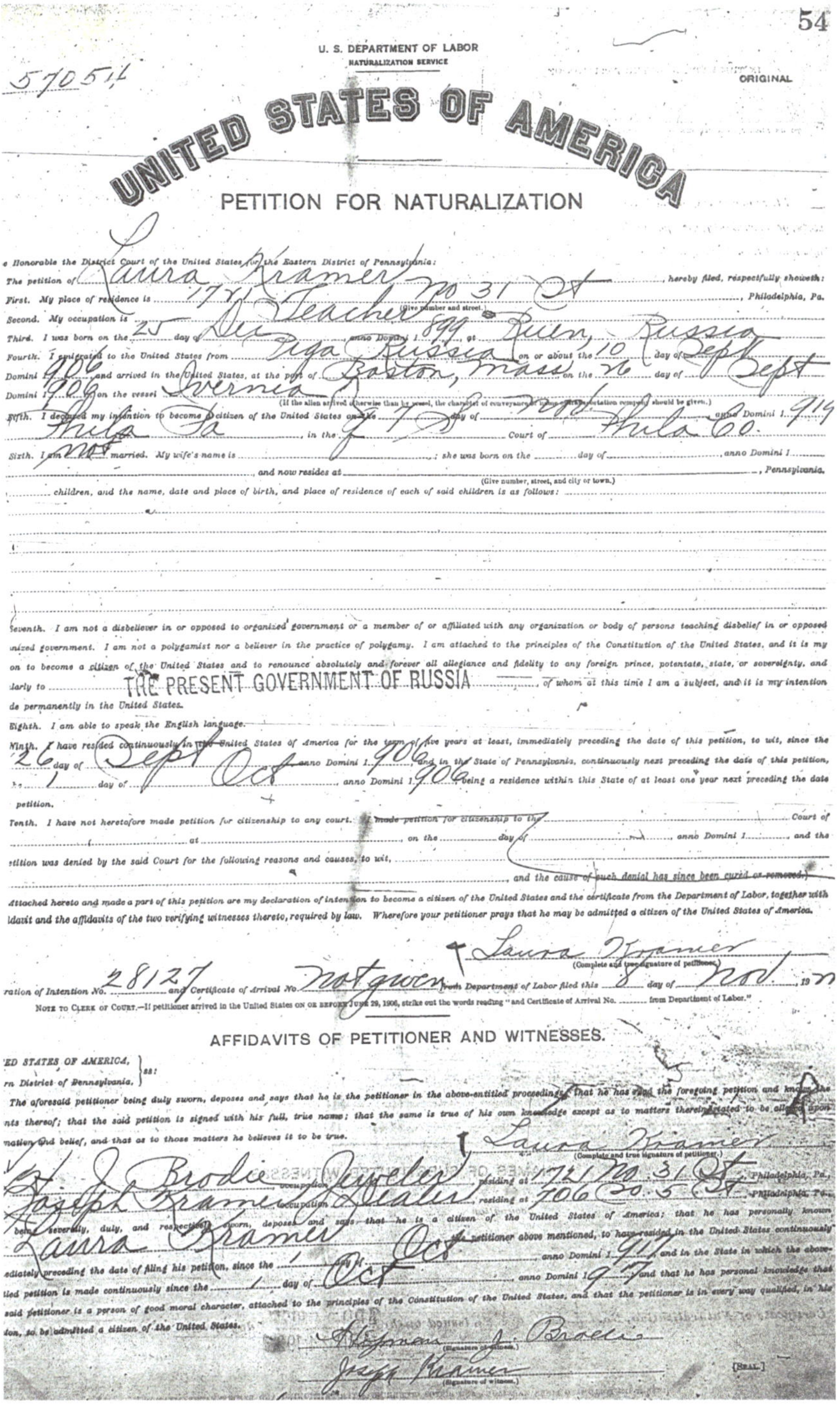

Appendix C: Death Certificate of Moses Kramer

H105.905 REV.(01/03)

This is to certify that this is a true copy of the record which is on file in the Pennsylvania Division of Vital Records in accordance with Act 66, P.L. 304, approved by the General Assembly, June 29, 1953.

WARNING: It is illegal to duplicate this copy by photostat or photograph.

Charles Hardester
Charles Hardester
State Registrar

3105027

No.

FEB 05 2004

Date

Certificate of death (faded photostat). Partially legible fields:

PLACE OF DEATH. County of PHILADELPHIA. City of PHILADELPHIA. Mt. Sinai Hospital.
CERTIFICATE OF DEATH. DEPARTMENT OF HEALTH, Bureau of Vital Statistics. Registration District No. 19. File No. 65905.
FULL NAME: Moses Kramer.
SEX: M. COLOR OR RACE: W. SINGLE, MARRIED, WIDOWED OR DIVORCED: Married.
DATE OF BIRTH: July 21, 1874. AGE: 48.
BIRTHPLACE: Russia. NAME OF FATHER: Joel. BIRTHPLACE OF FATHER: Russia. MAIDEN NAME OF MOTHER: Ankwan.
DATE OF DEATH: July 31, 1922.
CAUSE OF DEATH: Uremia. Contributory: Acute Retention of urine.
Informant: Benjamin Kramer.
Local Registrar: AUG 1922.

108

A LEGACY

Appendix D: Oath of Allegiance

IN THE MATTER OF THE PETITION OF

Laura Kramer

TO BE ADMITTED A CITIZEN OF THE UNITED STATES OF AMERICA.

Filed _____ Nov 8 ___, 19__

OATH OF ALLEGIANCE

I hereby declare, on oath, that I absolutely and entirely renounce and abjure all allegiance and fidelity to any foreign prince, potentate, state, or sovereignty, and particularly to ___ THE PRESENT GOVERNMENT OF RUSSIA ___ of whom I have heretofore been a subject; that I will support and defend the Constitution and laws of the United States of America against all enemies, foreign and domestic; and that I will bear true faith and allegiance to the same.

Laura Kramer

Subscribed and sworn to before me, in open Court, this **APR 24 1923** day of _____ A. D. 19___

J. O. Saub, Deputy Clerk.

NOTE.—In renunciation of title of nobility, add the following to the oath of allegiance before it is executed: "I further renounce the title of (give title), an order of nobility, which I have heretofore held."

ORDER OF COURT ADMITTING PETITIONER

Upon consideration of the petition of *Laura Kramer* _____ and affidavits in support thereof, and further testimony taken in open Court, it is ordered that the said petitioner, who has taken the oath required by law, be, and hereby is, admitted to become a citizen of the United States of America, this **APR 24 1923** day of _____, A. D. 19___

(It is further ordered, upon consideration of the petition of the said _____, that his name be, and hereby is, changed to _____, under authority of the provisions of section 6 of the act approved June 29, 1906 (34 Stat. L., pt. I, p. 596), as amended by the act approved March 4, 1913, entitled "An act to create a Department of Labor.")

By the Court:

109

DO AS I DID

Appendix E: Death Certificate of Zipora Kramer

H105.905 REV.(01/03)

This is to certify that this is a true copy of the record which is on file in the Pennsylvania Division of Vital Records in accordance with Act 66, P.L. 304, approved by the General Assembly, June 29, 1953.

WARNING: It is illegal to duplicate this copy by photostat or photograph.

Charles Hardester
Charles Hardester
State Registrar

3105037
No.

FEB 05 2004
Date

110

Appendix F: National Archives and Records Administration

National Archives and Records Administration

NORTHEAST REGION (PITTSFIELD)
10 CONTE DRIVE
PITTSFIELD, MASSACHUSETTS 01201-8230
www.nara.gov/regional

October 12, 2005

Hannah Leiter
300 Madison Avenue
Scranton, PA 18519-2431

Dear Mrs. Leiter:

We have tried several avenues to locate your grandparents on either census or arrival records. Here is what we've found (and not found).

On the 1900 census in Boston, we find a Feivell Mrinyx, age 25, born April 1875 in Russia, wife Sarah, age 26, born Jan 1874, married 5 years, 3 children all living, sons Soloman, born April 1897, Max born June 1898, and Morrle born Jan. 1900. It says that Feivell arrived in 1894 (he's a butcher) and Sarah arrived in 1895. We believe this is the correct family.

OFFICE OF REGIONAL RECORDS SERVICES

APPENDIX G: Ellis Island Foundation Passenger Records and Ship Manifest

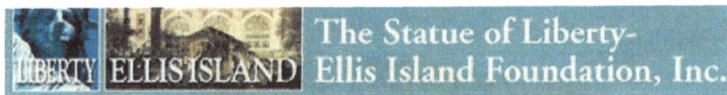

The Statue of Liberty-
ELLIS ISLAND **Ellis Island Foundation, Inc.**

Wel
Shop

▸ Passenger   ▸ Original Ship   ▸ Ship   ▸ View   ▸ Create an   ▸ Back to
Record   Manifest   Annotations   Annotation   Search
Results

SHIP MANIFEST

Manifests often extend over more than one page. Your passenger may be listed in this page, or a few pages forward or back. To see other pages in the manifest, click "previous" or "next." To save or purchase, click "View Original Manifest."

Fredrich der Grosse

VIEW ORIGINAL MANIFEST

Associated Passenger	Date of Arrival	Port of Departure	Line #	Page #	0098
Rumianek, Abram	Aug 26, 1903	Bremen	-	previous	next
				Original page	

Manifest for Fredrich der Grosse
Sailing from Bremen

Name	Gender	Age	Married	Ethnicity	Place of Residence
0001. Rezac, Rudolf	M	25y	S	Austr.	Nurschan
0002. Storek, Vincent	M	30y	M	Bohemia	Kladno
0003. Kopecky, Franz	M	25y	S	Bohemia	Cervene Janovice
0004. Valchar, Karoline	F	14y	S	Bohemia	Kutna Hora
0005. Faltejsek, Josef	M	36y	M	Bohemia	Boh. Rothwasser
0006. Faltejsek, Anna	F	39y	M	Bohemia	Boh. Rothwasser
0007. Nyiczik, Janos	M	32y	M	Hungary	Nadasd
0008. Dudas, Jozef	M	11y	S	Hungary	Nadasd
0009. Moskovits, Fanny	F	17y	S	Hungary	Kiszte
0010. Basala, Zuzanna	F	17y	S	Hungary	Dedasocz
0011. Pataki, Julianna	F	20y	S	Hungary	Karos
0012. Zera, Aniela	F	19y	S	Austria	Hrehorow
0013. Sroka, Anna	F	15y	S	Austria	Mokre
0014. Zural, Jewka	F	23y	S	Austria	Bielanka
0015. Zapur, Julianna	F	22y	S	Austria	Sowina
0016. Zaremba, Katarzyna	F	25y	M	Austria	Pien
0017. Zaremba, Mieczyslaw	M	9m	S	Austria	Pien
0018. Rumianek, Abram	M	27y	S	Russia	Mlawa
0019. Hammerl, Anna	F	23y	S	German	Rogging, By
0020. Hammerl, Franciska	F	19y	S	German	Rogging, By
0021. Huber, Joseph	M	20y	S	German	Pfolkofen, By.
0022. Weigl, Maria	F	28y	S	German	Holkbofen, By.
0023. Frammer, Gertrude	F	37y	S	German	Regensburg, By.
0024. Priller, Georg	M	25y	S	German	Geisenfeld, By.
0025. Puchta, Bernhard	M	18y	S	German	Stammbach
0026. Puchta, Martin	M	26y	S	German	Stammbach
0027. Weckert, Mathilda	F	48y	M	U.S.C.	Albany, N.Y.
0028. Weckart, Philipp	M	11y	S	U.S.C.	Albany, N.Y.
0029. Weigand, Matthaus	M	24y	S	German	Brendlorenzen, By.

Appendix H: Ellis Island Foundation Passenger Records

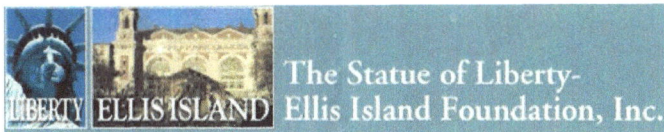

The Statue of Liberty-
ELLIS ISLAND Ellis Island Foundation, Inc.

► SIGN OUT
► T
Welcome,
Shopping

► Passenger Record | ► Original Ship Manifest | ► Ship | ► View Annotations | ► Create an Annotation | ► Back to Search Results

PASSENGER RECORD

RECENTLY UPDATED FEATURE!

Here is the record for the passenger. Click the links on the left to see more information about this passenger.

First Name:	Feiwel
Last Name:	Mintz
Ethnicity:	Russia
Last Place of Residence:	Penschnitz
Date of Arrival:	Jan 02, 1892
Age at Arrival: 22y Gender: M Marital Status:	
Ship of Travel:	Rhynland
Port of Departure:	Antwerp
Manifest Line Number:	0187

Appendix I: Ellis Island Foundation Ship Manifest

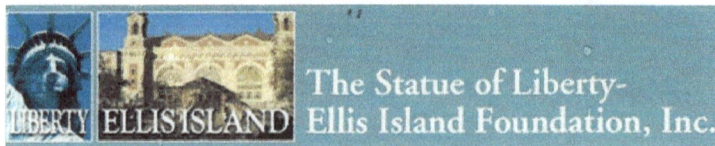

The Statue of Liberty-
Ellis Island Foundation, Inc.

▶ Passenger Record ▶ Original Ship Manifest ▶ Ship ▶ View Annotations ▶ Create an Annotation ▶ Back to Search Results

SHIP MANIFEST

Manifests often extend over more than one page. Your passenger may be listed in this page, or a few pages forward or back. To see other pages in the manifest, click "previous" or "next." To save or purchase, click "View Original Manifest."

Rhynland

VIEW ORIGINAL MANIFEST

Associated Passenger	Date of Arrival	Port of Departure	Line #	Page #	0757
Mintz, Feiwel	Jan 02, 1892	Antwerp	-	previous	next
				Original page	

Manifest for Rhynland
Sailing from Antwerp

Name	Gender	Age	Married	Ethnicity	Place of Residence
0163. Jonas, Kalenyock	M	28y		Hungary	Hetfouta
0164. Nuderko, Ila	F	25y		Hungary	Csermerns
0165. Nuderko, Gyura	F	3y		Hungary	Csermerns
0166. Nuderko, Maresa	F	1y		Hungary	Csermerns
0167. Szarman, Andreas	M	33y		Hungary	Bisztrieza
0168. Tilip, Franz Misck	M	43y		Hungary	Bisztrieza
0169. Bartek, Matyey	M	29y		Hungary	Bisztrieza
0170. Bartos, Miso	M	25y		Hungary	Kokava
0171. Jonas, Oravecz	M	35y		Hungary	Kokava
0172. Caja, Adam	M	28y		Hungary	Kokava
0173. Halasz, Andras	M	25y		Hungary	Pola
0174. Varga, Ivan	M	32y		Hungary	Pola
0175. Varga, Gyorgy	M	39y		Hungary	Pola
0176. Csucsko, Ferencz	M	19y		Hungary	Pola
0177. Szoke, Gyorgy	M	26y		Hungary	Farrs Easco
0178. Janosik, Gyorgy	M	17y		Hungary	Farrs Easco
0179. Takacz, Erzsebet	F	28y		Hungary	Palagy
0180. Szaszkevicz, Ivan	M	26y		Galizven	Garzonka
0181. Szverek, Tunko	M	26y		Galizven	Garzanka
0182. Benicszezak, Olekoa	M	26y		Galizven	Garzanka
0183. Nemeth, Gyorgy	M	44y		Hungary	Morrok
0184. Jonas, Bilig	M	27y		Hungary	Morrok
0185. Elpern, Jacob	M	22y		Russia	Thowns
0186. Elpern, Nechame	F	20y		Russian	Thowns
0187. Mintz, Feiwel	M	22y		Russia	Penschnitz
0188. Ivlosowitz, Hirsch	M	26y		Russia	Mlawa
0189. Milkewitz, Hmalle	F	30y		Russia	Dradzilow
0190. Milkewitz, Benjamin	M	12y		Russia	Dradzilow
0191. Milkewitz, Iner	M	10y		Russia	Dradzilow

Appendix J: Birth Certificate of Sam Mintz

HOTEL CASEY

"Scranton's Newest Modern Hotel"

FIREPROOF RAMP GARAGE CONVENIENT

SCRANTON 3, PENNA.

LACKAWANNA & ADAMS AVENUES

Sunday, February 24, 1952

Dear Mr. and Mrs. Mintz,

Believe me, I could not possibly find words to describe the pleasure of my experience in joining with you in the observance of the Sabbath at your home.

I would not have missed this opportunity and I am sincerely grateful that the Good Lord granted me the opportunity to be there.

If more people would open their homes and hearts as you people so sincerely do then brotherhood would be extended far beyond the guise of Brotherhood Week.

It makes me indeed happy to know wonderful folks like you.

"Stop at Recognized Hotels"

Appendix K: Letter from Mr. Ditchett

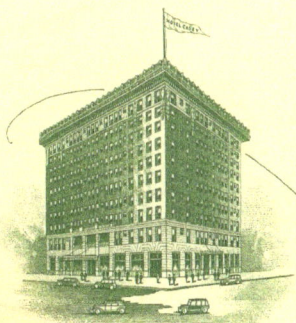

May the Good Lord bless you all and grant you long, happy and healthy lives and may good fortune always smile upon your lovely home.

Very sincerely yours

Edwin S. Ditchett

APPENDIX L: Letter from Executive Director of Jewish Home

The Jewish Home

בית יתומים ומושב זקנים

712 HARRISON AVENUE

SCRANTON 10, PA.

ROSLYN B. BURNAT
EXECUTIVE DIRECTOR

May 14th
19   47

Miss Hannah Mintz
304 North Webster Avenue
Scranton, Pa.

Dear Hannah:

We want to thank you very much for your most generous Mother's
Day donation. This was the nicest and most appreciative
donation that our folks received and helped them to gain the
full spirit of Mother's Day. We know this was some sacrifice
to you and we hope that you will be rewarded many times over
for your kindness.

Our folks pray that the Lord shall bestow his blessings upon
you and each and everyone of them thanks you from the bottom
of their hearts.

Most sincerely yours,

THE JEWISH HOME

Roslyh B. Burnat
Executive Director

RBB:HM

Appendix M: Letters of Condolence from Abe and Simeon Guterman

415 MADISON AVENUE
NEW YORK 17, N.Y.

February 25, 1964

Mrs. Sam Mintz
300 Madison Avenue
Scranton, Penna.

Dear Mrs. Mintz:

I was deeply grieved to learn that Sam had passed away and extend to you and the entire family my heartfelt condolences.

I knew Sam from the time when I was a very young child and always had a great affection for him. He was always a kindly and considerate person and even as a child I was impressed with his gentility. I can still recall the many times when he would take me in his Model T Ford coupe to deliver meat to various customers in town. I used to spend many pleasant hours with him as a child both on these delivery trips and in the butcher shop itself which was located, as you know, not far from where we lived.

Although in later years I would only see him occasionally when I would visit Scranton I continued to have a fondness and regard for him. The Scranton scene will not be the same without him.

Although I know that mere words may be small solace in the loss of a near

119

Appendix M: Letters of Condolence from Abe and Simeon Guterman

415 MADISON AVENUE
NEW YORK 17, N.Y.   2/25/64

Page 2

and dear one, it may be some consolation
to you and the family to know the high
regard in which he was held and that he
will continue to live in the hearts and
minds of those who had the good fortune
of counting him as a friend.

Sincerely yours,

Abraham S. Guterman

Appendix M: Letters of Condolence from Abe and Simeon Guterman

SIMEON L. GUTERMAN

511 WEST 232 STREET, NEW YORK 63, N. Y.

February 16, 1964

Dear Mrs. Mintz

It is with a sense of shock and of grief, as of a member of the immediate family, that I write to you on the passing of your husband. Our visits to Scranton were always gladdened by the all too brief contacts with Sam. For Sam stood for a number of things that are rare and beautiful when we find them embodied in one person. He was a Jew in the highest sense of the term, he was an ethical and moral being, beyond the measure normally accorded to mortals. I am sure that I express the sentiments of all who have known Sam. It will be a source of solace to you and to your dear family to have lived with and

APPENDIX M: Letters of Condolence from Abe and Simeon Guterman

know this wonderful person. May
God console you all; as your friends
will try to do.

In condolence,

Simeon J. Guterman